SHADES *of* PUBLIC FINANCE

VOLUME TWO

More Insider Stories of the Municipal Bonds that Built America

Richard Land Sigal

DUDLEY COURT PRESS
SONOITA, AZ

Published in the United States of America by
Dudley Court Press
PO Box 102 Sonoita, AZ 85637
www.DudleyCourtPress.com

Cover and interior design by Dunn+Associates, www.Dunn-Design.com

Publisher's Cataloging-in-Publication Data
Names: Sigal, Richard Land, author.
Title: Shades of public finance / Richard Land Sigal.
Description: Sonoita : Dudley Court Press, LLC, [2020]
Contents: vol. 1. Illicit bankrutpcies, innovative municipal bonds, and why the patriots didn't move to Hartford
Contents vol. 2. More insider stories of the municipal bonds that built America.
Identifiers: ISBN: 978-1-940013-66-4 (v. 1 : paperback) | 978-1-940013-73-2 (v.2 : paperback)
978-1-940013-61-9 (v.1 : ebook) | 978-1-940013-62-6 (v. 2 : ebook)
978-1-940013-74-9 (v.1 : audio) | 978-1-940013-75-6 (v. 2 : audio)
LCCN: 2019921137 (v. 1) | 2019921092 (v. 2)
Subjects: LCSH: Municipal bonds—Law and legislation--United States. | Bond market—United States.
Bond market—United States—History. | Municipal finance—United States. | Local finance—United States.
BISAC: BUSINESS & ECONOMICS / Public Finance. | BUSINESS & ECONOMICS / Finance / General.
BUSINESS & ECONOMICS / Economic History. | BUSINESS & ECONOMICS / Skills.
Classification: LCC: KF6775 .S54 2020 | DDC: 346.73/0922--dc23

Look for other books in this series at your favorite bookseller
or at www.DudleyCourtPress.com

CONTENTS

PREFACE

In *Shades of Public Finance, Volume 2,* I am pleased to recount some of the most innovative infrastructure financings that either happened or were waylaid by politics or officious interlopers and to explore the concept of reciprocal bond tax-exempt between federal and state governments.

Ever since levying an income tax became federal and state law, the market for tax-exempt bonds has created unique opportunities for states, public authorities and municipalities, wealthy individuals, and investment trust fund managers attracted to interest rate incentives and safety features of those bonds.

Unfortunately, when President John F. Kennedy's Department of Treasury developed a scoring system to manage the federal budget, it didn't account for how that system would affect local budgets. For example, this scoring shibboleth was in play in the Tax Cuts and Jobs Act signed by President Donald Trump on December 22, 2017. This legislation shut down a multibillion-dollar tax-exempt refunding bond program that reduced significantly state and local budget and thus tax relief. Presently, the National Association of State Treasurers has as its highest legislative priority the repeal of the relevant provision because the continued low interest rate bond market is ripe for refunding outstanding bonds bearing much higher interest rates. Thus there remains a need for balancing federal/state sovereignty in public financing tools. Several chapters in this book awaken you to the tension created in finding that balance.

By reading both Volume 1 and Volume 2, you'll be able to appreciate public financing's substantial impact on public resources*. Pay particular attention in this Volume 2 to the notorious *Kelo v. City of New London* case in Chapter 7. It is analyzed by me, an insider, using real facts rather than the propaganda put out by interlopers looking for the limelight—those who flamed a fight that was wasteful since the issue had already been settled twenty years before in a fully reasoned decision by the Supreme Court of the United States. The waste of time, opportunities, and taxpayers' money has not yet been retrievable because the recession and corporate policy changed the feasibility of the plan.

While Chapter 7 describes the shady side of public finance that harms taxpayers and communities, you'll find most chapters in Volume 2 reveal the best examples of municipal bonds that have been building America for three centuries. They offer much from which to learn. Read on!

**Please note that in Volume 1, the Puerto Rico chapters are incomplete due to the news changing daily about the territory's ongoing fiscal and political problems. Updates will be provided in a planned third volume. Perhaps by that publication, fiscal and political resolution benefitting the taxpayer residents of that island will prevail.*

INTRODUCTION

If you have read Shades of Public Finance, Volume 1, this introduction may be somewhat repetitious. If you have preferred to start in reverse order with this *Shades of Public Finance,* Volume 2, welcome to learning about these important issues in public finance: clean water, solid waste disposal, highways, utilities, open space, gambling and native Americans, public authorities, reciprocal tax immunity, and eminent domain. You may not realize it, but these topics reside in the shadows of your everyday life and budget.

Reading the chapters here, particularly those revealing innovative public finance solutions over the years, should provide you with confidence that your state and local officials get it right at least some of the time. Knowing what goes on will help you become a knowledgeable citizen and taxpayer. The chapters in this book bring these matters into the sunlight for better or for worse. And you'll see how certain individuals and institutions disregard the interests of taxpayers for personal greed or for political/business bias.

Although public finance might be a subject that's new to you, it is fascinating because of its direct effect on everyday life, though always in its shadows. On the one hand, bathroom and kitchen waste disposal, potholes, local taxes, corruption, and illicit activities as well as federal action, bankruptcy consultants, and corporate greed make issues in public finance relevant to your every activity and budget. On the other hand, state initiatives, taxpayer needs, and creative financings move our communities ahead—many made possible through public finance.

Both Volume 1 and this Volume 2 feature a balanced mixture of topics that expose the real life of public finance without redundancy or repetition. Together, they provide insights into public finance in many regions of the United States ranging from Alaska to Puerto Rico. Specifically, this volume highlights the tax policy tension between the sovereign states and the sovereign federal government. It highlights the efforts by the Supreme Court of the United States (SCOTUS) to properly balance the treatment of interest income under state and federal personal income taxation. Chapter 7 explains the deleterious result of an officious interference by outliers that delayed a legal (under both federal and state constitutions) "taking" of property in a Connecticut condemnation case. It has already cost resident taxpayers many years of real estate tax benefits despite the highest court in the land reaffirming a precedent. Such outliers in the cause of libertarianism are on a national campaign spreading fictional fears. In each state, they're promoting statutory amendments to stop those remedial economic development necessities from benefiting you and your community.

Having an informed citizenry is essential, particularly in these times. This Volume 2, like Volume 1, features chapters that lift the blinds on the shady side of public finance and encourage you to enjoy, appreciate, and gain insight from each.

Part One

Politics vs. Economics in Public Finance

CHAPTER 1

What Happens When Local Politics Win?

This chapter recounts how the financial affairs of a major municipality can be controlled and impaired by the financial interests of the rich and powerful.

In early December 1978, my client, John Carhuff, the head of public finance at First Boston, retained me to travel with him to Cleveland. I was to counsel First Boston in preparing Cleveland's mayor to negotiate for renewal of fourteen million dollars' worth of notes held by the local banks.

While Cleveland was then considered a city with declining business and population like Buffalo, the small amount of the required renewal seemed easily achievable. However, on the plane going there, John explained that, in representing Mayor Dennis Kucinich, we would be representing a person who was considered an outsider with a small loyal supporting staff. Knowing more was at stake than only note renewal, I sensed we were in for a tough negotiating battle.

By way of background, the private utility, Cleveland Electric Utility Company (CEUC), had allegedly been violating antitrust rules numerous times.[1]

Specifically, it had been attempting to put the public utility, Municipal Light, out of business. Over time, Municipal Light had accrued fourteen million dollars in debt, which Mayor Kucinich's predecessor had sought to settle by selling Municipal Light to CEUC. This would resolve the debt and thus settle the antitrust suit.

When Mayor Kucinich was elected, he reversed course, seeking other means to pay off that debt while proceeding with the antitrust suit against CEUC.[2] The mayor was adamant and outspoken to the effect that the antitrust case was a separate matter with a solid claim for substantial damages, so he was unwilling to engage in any settlement talks linked to the small amount of renewal of the notes.

Efforts Stymied

However, Mayor Kucinich's efforts were stymied by Ohio's largest bank (whose ownership was, I was informed, entangled with CEUC) and by Cleveland's city council. In those years, it could be assumed with good reason that the powerful and rich families in Cleveland were owners of stock in CEUC. In those days, the IOUs (investor-owned utilities) were regulated with reasonably attractive rates of return and considered safe and prudent investments, so every family trust would have included a substantial holding of this IOU stock. However, the city's antitrust case seriously challenged its safety as an investment. That's why members of the city council, led by the filibuster of its speaker under control of his constituents—the rich and powerful citizens and their trusts—were holding up the authorization for note renewal.

I went to Cleveland in early December facing this political environment. In the first meeting with the banks, I was impressed by the vast amount of rich mahogany in the conference room and hallways. Cleveland had been home to major corporations, and the splendor of the downtown offices spoke volumes about the wealth that once made Cleveland among the richest cities in the nation. I was representing Buffalo as well at the time, and Cleveland clearly had the benefit of many more corporate headquarters and centers of industrial power than Buffalo.

Next, I noted that the traditional bond counsel firms were not represented in the room due to conflicts of interest with various clients. In particular, Squire Dempsey, the leading bond counsel firm, found itself squarely on both sides, having represented the city in the past as its bond counsel and as counsel to CEUC, the investor-owned utility. This IOU was in door-to-door competition with the city-owned municipal light company against which the city had filed a treble damage antitrust case.[3]

John Carhuff of First Boston made it clear to the banks that Cleveland's fiscal problems extended well beyond the note renewal. He said the city should successfully renew its notes and then the city and city council could address resolving the lawsuit. Therefore, be advised that they should get the note deal done and then resolve all the other issues as part of an overall restructuring plan. On December 14th, I spent the evening negotiating this approach with the bankers at the same time as the mayor and his staff were working city council members to pass the renewal resolution.

Refused to Yield the Floor

The city council's spokesperson, George Forbes, held the floor from approximately ten p.m. until well past midnight. He refused to yield it to present the renewal resolution for introduction and voting. As a result, at midnight, the relatively small number of notes went into default. As the largest municipal default in history since the depression, it became headline news throughout the nation.[4] It is unclear for how long Cleveland paid a penalty in its tax-exempt interest rate, but clearly it paid something. For instance, some blue sky laws prevent buying bonds of a defaulted issuer for a period of five years.

Then what? Mayor Kucinich was defeated at the next election. His successor not only dropped the case but went on to become governor. However, to Mayor Kucinich's credit, the press and citizenry recognized that he had been absolutely correct in his position regarding the interests of the taxpayers. In 1997, Kucinich was elected to the U.S. House of Representatives and was regularly reelected through 2013. He was twice a candidate for U.S. president and ran for governor in Ohio.

What's the takeaway from this Cleveland default? That despite the mayor's leadership and astute understanding of the validity and value of the antitrust claims, vested financial interests allowed the city to default on its indebtedness. This resulted in increased interest costs to city taxpayers and the budget loss of the enormous benefit of an achievable award in the antitrust case.

However, this local political power of private interests over public interests was "small time" compared to the political power that was persuasive in a national agenda to protect (think "scam") the special interest of investor-owned utilities that operated nuclear facilities. Those investor-owned facilities convinced legislatures in several states to deregulate the power production part of the utility business and issue taxable so-called rate reduction bonds to absorb the stranded costs of those power facilities. These terms and the "deregulation mania" that swept the country is described in the next chapter.

CHAPTER 2

Who Cares about Ratepayers?

One disappointment of practicing public finance is finding that the interest of the taxpayer or ratepayer is often not the foremost motivation in structuring programs. This chapter illustrates a shady case in which several investment banks and investor-owned utilities (IOUs) successfully fought against a bond program that could have been issued as tax exempt. Because of their efforts, millions of dollars in interest were added to utility bills and paid by the ratepayers.

My first experience in working with investor-owned utilities (IOUs) occurred when the U.S. Congress was eager to clean up the water flow in this country.

Congress, through the Environmental Protection Agency legislation, was mandating companies to install pollution control devices in piping before disposing of industrial waste into the rivers and lakes and had statutorily provided a financing incentive to encourage compliance. An amendment to Section 103 of the Internal Revenue Code allowed pollution control bonds to be issued on behalf of private companies and IOUs by special-purpose public entities. The interest on these Pollution Control Bonds was exempt from federal income taxation.

My friends Jimmy Lopp and Dick Locke from EF Hutton were the leading bankers promoting the legislation and thereafter underwriting the tax-exempt bonds. (Georgia Pacific, DuPont, IBM, Northeast Utilities, and Exxon were just a few of the big-name companies for which Hawkins served as bond counsel.) These bonds would be used to finance pollution-control equipment at their corporate or utility plants.

Under the amendment—whether it pertained to coal-fired plants, nuclear plants, paper mills, or even the Alaska pipeline—anything directly attributable to a construction cost and installation of pollution control equipment could be financed with tax-exempt bonds issued through a state development agency.

In the 1980s, billions of those bonds were issued by almost every state. I mention this to highlight that the IOUs were familiar with working through a state bonding authority. They had taken advantage of the tax-exempt interest rate incentive by participating in a tax-exempt governmental bonding program. That allowed rates to be lower for their customers (the ratepayers) than if they had issued taxable bonds in order to address the pollution control mandate imposed on them.

Edison Institute and Enron

IOUs have an organized lobby and support organization known as the Edison Institute. Due in part to the dynamics of the development of "virtual" utilities led by the Enron Corporation, the concept of deregulating the utility industry became popular state by state—supported, stimulated, energized, and lobbied for by this powerful Edison Institute.[5] The economics of pushing to deregulate the production and sale of electricity *but not the transmission of energy* is a complicated chess-like game. The IOUs developed this game primarily to sell off their nuclear power production plants, which required rates higher than competitive power contracts of coal facilities or virtual utilties. At the same time, they could retain and preserve their monopoly on transmission (for which there was no competition).

Enron (which later collapsed and whose officers were convicted of fraud) was created primarily as a "virtual" power company with purchase and delivery contracts as its assets. For the most part, Enron did not own any actual power production facilities or "hard assets." It bought power on a firm basis from power-producing utilities and then sold that power in an unfettered, unregulated way and at rates lower than allowed to be charged by nuclear investor-owned utilities by a state public utility commission.

The hard-owned-asset IOUs led by the Edison Institute determined they could only compete with Enron if the industry were deregulated subject to the conditions discussed here. The ratepayers would have to absorb the remaining "asset" on the IOU books already built into charges for paying off the remaining debt on bonds that had been issued for those power plants. That "asset" was called "stranded cost." The bonds to finance that cost were termed "rate reduction" bonds on the theory that after those bonds were paid off, that IOU's rates could be competitive and therefore reduced. To qualify as a capital investment, the acquisition of the present value of the "stranded cost" was deemed by statute as "transition property." The monthly charges to the ratepayers were mandated by statute as "irrevocable."

In other words, to compete in a deregulated market, the capital cost of constructing power plants needed to be repaid through both (1) the benefit of depreciation and (2) irrevocable rate charges. Theoretically, consumers could save money by buying power in a competitive (nonregulated) market made up of both "virtual" and "hard-wired" companies (or combinations thereof) in a free competitive market but not at a price fixed by the state public utility commission. If ratepayers were allowed such choice, then in "giving up" the regulated price regime, these IOUs were entitled to be compensated for the "stranded cost" of the power plants built under the regulated market. This was a fair *quid pro quo*, especially if the ratepayer bought into the concept of the vitality of such a competitive market.

Edison Institute led the lobbying for this in every state, requiring these rate reduction bonds to finance the "stranded costs" as a condition preceding deregulation.

Comparing states that did permit deregulation and issued rate reduction bonds to those that didn't, what happened? Did rates actually go down in those states permitting deregulation? Was it a fiction of economics by the Edison Institute to allow many of the IOUs to unload their outdated or overbuilt nuclear (or other) power plants? The answers are beyond the scope of this book.

In Connecticut, Northeast Utilities sold its nuclear facilities almost immediately after closing on its rate reduction bonds. The utility company that bought those facilities now advocates reinstating the public service commission rate-setting role. This is due to the cheaper and alternative cost of available gas, which has become so competitive with nuclear plants that the continuing business of owning and preserving nuclear power plants is at risk today. (The virtual power company of "Enron" vintage is, of course, extinct.)

Lower Interest Rate?

In Connecticut, I was retained by the state treasurer to review the deregulation legislation that had been introduced. My focus was on the original taxable bond structuring, not whether deregulation theory was voodoo economics or not. I advised the state's treasurer that the interest rate could be much lower. In my firm's opinion, tax-exempt bonds could be issued, and that difference in interest would result in a lower interest cost to the ratepayer.

Here was our analysis. The standard deregulation legislation being introduced in almost every state included an "irrevocable transition charge." It was mandated by that law to be added to the utility bill and payable regardless of actual use. It was also measured to be the exact amount of the annual amortization of principal and interest on the rate reduction bonds.

The legal analysis was simple: A "mandated charge" regardless of use meets the definition of a tax if it's imposed by a state and if the bonds were issued through a state entity. Therefore, the interest on such bonds would be tax exempt. One IOU, the United Illuminating Company serving the New Haven region, concluded in writing that my approach was correct. But I met an inexplicable resistance from the other Connecticut IOU (e.g., Northeast Utilities). Their leaders were adamantly fighting against that theory through utility lawyers and bankers.[6]

An explanation for this opposition is that these deals were very large. The IOUs and their corporate lawyers and investment bankers wanted to control the deals and the marketing profits derived from them. And they did not want the state treasurer to retain the consultants. For example, despite my being retained by the state's treasurer in Connecticut, Northeast Utilities hired three well-known consultants (including the former state majority leader), who successfully lobbied against and defeated my tax-exempt draft of the deregulation legislation. Each received $100,000 for that session of the legislature and, of course, the utilities also participate in contributing to the campaigns of the election officials.[7]

In addition, efforts led by Merrill Lynch and me to persuade utilities in Virginia, New York, South Carolina, California, and other states to issue their bonds on a tax-exempt basis were also rebuffed. The political "muscle" those utilities lobbyists have is well documented at the federal level in DC. At the state level, their lobbyists have become ubiquitous as well. (Enron, the leader of the push for deregulation, collapsed because it was a fraud in all respects.) Billions of rate reduction bonds were issued with taxable-interest bonds, thereby costing ratepayers millions over a tax-exempt interest rate.

Again, those deals in every state were done using taxable financing. However, my analysis has been proven correct. Today, states routinely issue bonds with a mandated charge on utility ratepayers to finance clean energy facilities and protect the credit of distressed utilities. For example, based on the tax views developed at Hawkins by me for those rate reduction bonds, legislators in New York extended the concept to benefit the Long Island Power Authority (LIPA). LIPA was in serious credit distress related to its ratepayers having to absorb the imbedded cost of financing the Shoreham nuclear plant that was shut down and mothballed because it lacked a nuclear disaster exit strategy. The state of New York amended the LIPA legislation to impose this irrevocable charge (tax). Thereafter, LIPA has issued billions of tax-exempt refunding bonds secured by such rate charge to refund its higher interest rate bonds that had originally been issued to finance the now closed facility.

Today, it is a recognized right of the state to mandate a charge on the use of home and commercial electrical energy for the purpose of enhancing the credit of a public power authority or to provide subsidies or grants to alternative power ventures such as windmills or solar panels for home or commercial use.

This rate reduction bond program is one of those enigmas about the municipal bond industry being subservient to and operating in the shadow of the corporate finance industry. Why were the rate reduction bonds issued as taxable when it could have been established that the mandated charge was a tax and thereby those bonds could have been issued at tax-exempt rates like had been done for the pollution control bonds? In my view, the voices of excellent bond and tax-exempt partners in large law firms and excellent investment bankers in public finance departments of investment banking firms were silenced by those organizations' corporate law and corporate utility partners because fees are much higher in corporate offerings than municipal offerings.[8]

In my case, undoubtedly it was the political power wielded by the largest public utility in Connecticut and its three lobbyists that prevented those bonds from being issued at tax-exempt rates. Clearly, the motivation supporting taxable rate reduction bonds wasn't in the best interests of the ratepayers. However, once political leaders realized it was acceptable to add charges to the rate base in order to develop wind, solar, and water alternative energy, it became a popular "alternative tax" to secure tax-exempt bonds.

CHAPTER 3

Which City Gets a Minor League Team?

This chapter relates the move of a Yankee farm baseball club from Albany, New York, to Norwich, Connecticut, over the objections of both Governor Mario Cuomo and Yankee owner George Steinbrenner. It provides an example of public finance and economic development combining to make a move like this attractive.

Considerable controversy has been written about whether a municipality should expend taxpayer money or use its bonding power to attract a sports team to play in town. My anecdotal experience with the Albany team moving to Norwich is that, despite published economic analysis to the contrary, taxpayers show that there is widespread acceptance for a professional team playing home games in their town as good business.

Here's some background. One fall day in 1994, my good friend and fellow Hawkins managing partner, Bob Rosenberg, called me to request that I contact Bob Friedman, a businessman who served on the board of his client, Nassau County Development Agency. On that call, Friedman said he was a joint owner of a minor baseball team, Albany Yankees, who were interested in moving the team to Connecticut.

For some of us who grew up in post–World War II and outside a major league baseball city, we remember attending (usually with one or both parents) minor league baseball games during spring and summer days. We even went at night to a field that had lights. We would surmise which player would make it to the big leagues or, in some cases, which player would be called back up to the majors. In all cases, we rooted hard for the local team and enjoyed the activity as a family. But before long, movies, drive-in theatres, television, and driving around became more popular pastimes than minor league baseball.

Today, still, despite video games and other distractions, minor league baseball survives in some towns as a local family activity.

Move the Team

Poor attendance for the minor team's home games in Albany over the years had caused the team's owners to explore moving it elsewhere. Freidman knew I was the bond counsel for the state of Connecticut, including its development authority. Perhaps Danbury near the New York border might be interested in welcoming a Yankee affiliate, he suggested. I told him two things, namely, that Connecticut residents were equally divided between Yankee and Red Sox fans, and that eastern Connecticut should be on his list of areas to consider. I fondly recalled attending minor league baseball games in New London where I spent summers at my grandparents' house. Then I asked around about interest. I found out that, in fact, a local real estate attorney from Norwich, Glenn Carberry, had researched the concept of attracting a minor league team to the area. He would be delighted to talk to the Albany Yankee franchise.

Carberry's plan worked out this way. Six neighboring towns—Norwich, New London, Groton, Waterford, Montville, and Mystic—would each designate a possible site in their town from which the team could choose. After that, all six towns would agree to support the teams's application to the state for tax increment financing (TIF)[9] by the Connecticut Development Authority. The TIF statute I had drafted allowed for a state guaranty of bonding if the tax revenue (whether sales, income, or property) generated by the venture was analyzed to be sufficient to pay debt service on the bonds to finance the infrastructure.

The team selected a site in Groton just off I-95 near the Mystic Aquarium and Mystic Seaport. It was considered the right spot to generate a local fan base as well as tourist dollars attracted to these other venues during the summer. An announcement was made about the choice to move the teams. Governor Mario Cuomo—who himself had been a baseball player in his day—went "crazy." No way would he allow the team to move from Albany. And he would make sure of it by talking to his kindred friend, George Steinbrenner, the tyrannical owner of the Yankees.

The team owners of this minor league team were extremely savvy and, of course, knew Steinbrenner well. They made it publicly known they were surprised by Governor Cuomo's "crazy" reaction. To their knowledge, the governor had never attended a home game in Albany. He had been asked to throw out the first ball of the season five years in a row and declined each time. Therefore, the owners had presumed the governor didn't care about the team playing in Albany.

By comparison, the owners made clear how welcoming the towns had been in Connecticut and that a new stadium with overwhelming community support and state financing was an attractive investment opportunity. They also anticipated that, to avoid a breach with Cuomo, Steinbrenner would publicly object, but that the league would allow the move to happen.

Norwich's Turn

However, it turned out the park site picked in Groton had been trusted to the town. The trustees of the foundation that had made the gift determined that a commercial venture of a minor league stadium on land dedicated for recreational use was not permitted under the trust. Within a week of this setback, the city of Norwich authorized its $500,000 grant to buy an available site to house the stadium in the Norwich Industrial Park. The fact that Glenn Carberry lived in Norwich was critical to the quick reaction by that city. The team owners immediately accepted this, and the move was on.[10]

George Steinbrenner abstained in the voting in the league's approval of the move. Governor Cuomo voiced his complaints, but his failure over the years to support the team was well known. Neither the city of Albany nor the state of New York marshalled any effort to counteroffer.

The TIF financing was successful, and Dodd Stadium in Norwich became the home of the Yankee affiliate. The team, the Norwich Navigators, had a successful ten-year run and then, after attendance lagged, moved to Trenton, New Jersey. Another major league affiliate was lured to replace this Yankee's minor league team.

Fortunately for the state, the tax increment sales tax was sufficient to cover the debt service on the bonds, but barely. As was discussed in Volume 1 in the chapter about the New England Patriots' proposed move to Hartford, the relocation of a sports team generates fascinating economic and political dynamics.

Part Two

Schemes and Scams in Public Finance

CHAPTER 4

Who Are the Bad Guys?

Activities involving elected officials and public finance officials in sophisticated schemes might seem superficial on their face—business as usual—but in fact can be illegal. The chapters that follow depict several of those situations and other examples of unethical or shoddy behavior that, while not criminal, were clearly wrong or revealed poor policy.

Despite popular perception, most politicians run for office to provide public service. That is also true of public finance professionals, whether it be those who work for the agencies rating the bonds, the lawyers who counsel the issuers, the financial folks who are the financial advisors, the underwriters or insurers of the bonds, or the accountants who review and audit the numbers. Compensation is considerably less for those in public finance than for their compatriots in corporate finance. Corporate clients' incomes can be significant, and they are able to pay up for specialized advice.

Yet, as in corporate finance from the 1960s on, there were several instances of criminal activities involving elected officials and public finance officials in sophisticated schemes. During my career, I had the misfortune to come across people who chose the public finance field because they thought money could be made by *appearing to play by the rules* but actually engaging in illegal activities. Here are some examples.

Paul Silvester

Paul Silvester was appointed deputy treasurer in Connecticut by Treasurer Chris Burnham, the first elected Republican in a while in that office. Paul was born in Hartford to a fine family of lawyers but chose to start as an investment banker. He told me that his outspokenness and lack of listening skills came from being the youngest of several brothers. He always had to interrupt and command attention to make his voice heard. Extremely smart, he provided excellent suggestions at board meetings but lacked the ability to communicate them well.

The treasurer's office in Connecticut manages the investment of the state employees' pension fund. Customarily, someone whose fund was accepted for pension funds investing by the treasurer and oversight committee would pay a finder's fee to the person who introduced the fund manager to the treasurer. This finder's fee, about 1 percent annually of the amount involved, historically had been an honest way to attract worthy investment options.

However, Paul decided to game that system by first steering those fund applicants to a friend of his. That friend would make the appointment with Paul and would then split the fee and kick back a portion to Paul. But it didn't work. Paul was caught, tried, and jailed for doing this.[11] A similar fate for comparable criminal activity awaited Alan Hevesi after he had been elected and was serving as New York State comptroller.[12]

What astonishes me is that the Silvester case was in all the newspapers, including in New York, because it included shenanigans with his mistress[13] and the prosecution of the former majority leader in the Senate, William DiBella. DiBella was the beneficiary of the steering and was fined almost a million dollars.[14]

Hevesi should have been aware of this scheme and realized his similar steering would be noticed and prosecuted. Paul, as the deputy state treasurer, served on several of the boards of the authorities for which I was bond counsel. Fortunately, he never approached me on bond financings to participate in any kickback scheme. In fact, despite having cocktails after a meeting with Paul, I was explicitly excluded from joining a special dinner thereafter with his co-conspirators.

Arthur Abba Goldberg

Another scheme that almost implicated Hawkins involved Arthur Abba Goldberg, a founding partner at the investment banking firm of Matthews & Wright. It specialized in doing bond financing for low and moderate-cost housing projects.

During the 1980s, the statute regulating tax-exempt financing for these projects authorized the U.S. Treasury to write regulations as it deemed necessary. Those regulations would ban certain financing structures unless the bond issue closed by the end of the calendar year. It seemed every year during the 1980s, as new regulations were promulgated, we were closing many deals during Christmas week. We had the pressure that if the deal we were working on did not close by year end, it could not be done. Then if it could be restructured, it would have to be issued under the new tax rules, or it would just have to be issued as a taxable financing at a higher interest rate. In most cases, that would mean the deal was dead because the feasibility of the project depended on tax-exempt bond rates.

Arthur's firm was thinly capitalized and could not afford to buy and carry an inventory of bonds. Also, it did not have a line of credit with which to buy the bonds of several of his deals at the year-end closing and then repay the line upon resale of the bonds the following year.[15] In other words, his firm needed to have resold those bonds to investors simultaneously with the closing and therefore to have purchased the bonds with good funds on the day of closing.

With the pressure of so many bond issues closing at year end, he devised a scheme whereby he provided a bank check at the December 31 closing that had "allowed" the bond issue to close by the end of the year. In fact, the cashier's check was a scam, as it was certified by his "shell" bank in Saipan. As a result, Arthur pleaded guilty to three counts of mail fraud in California and one count of conspiracy to defraud in Illinois.[16]

Arthur Abba Goldberg proved to be a scam artist of note. After he was released from prison, he embarked on and was reportedly in another scan involving fund raising for conversion therapy, luckily not in the public finance practice.

Fortunately for me, we were retained and scheduled to close at year end on one of Arthur's housing deals. I had challenged one of the developers about the excessive development fees being charged. Because that extensive discussion was delaying the documentation process, I suggested the developer find other counsel (if he really needed to close the deal by year end), which he did.

Of course, it was one of the deals that closed with a "kited" check. I often wonder if I would have questioned the reality of that offshore bank if I had been at the closing that New Year's Eve.

Governor John Rowland

Other bad guys I have known include Governor John Rowland of Connecticut, but to his credit, despite billions of dollars in bond issues under his three four-year terms, there wasn't a whiff of bond scandal or money illegally passing on these deals.

Governor Rowland was from Waterbury, Connecticut. John was jailed after winning his third term as governor because the local plumber installed a hot tub for free in his summer home (just one out of multiple misdeeds).[17] On a positive note, his terms as governor were marked for his successful efforts to rebuild Connecticut cities and preserve the venues for arts in the cities.[18]

In addition to these public figures who were convicted of criminal activity, some had a manner of practice that could be considered unethical. One example occurred early in my career. That's when I learned that public officials with stellar reputations and positions were not always trustworthy.

Arthur Levitt Jr.

Arthur Levitt Jr. was the son of State Comptroller Arthur Levitt Sr. of New York. Levitt Senior presided as the barb on the conscience of Governor Nelson Rockefeller in circumventing the referendum requirement by creating conduit bond financing structures to build state office facilities (the Albany Mall) or housing projects financed by Authority bonds and backed by the state's so-called "moral obligation."

Levitt Junior grew up in the household featuring both public service and public finance as dinner conversations. At the time of this episode, Levitt Junior was the president of the American Stock Exchange (AMEX). In this role, he let it be known he was considering relocating the facility from its antiquated quarters behind Trinity Church in lower Manhattan and would modernize its trading equipment. The Exchange was then home to small cap companies (compared to the major corporations on the New York Stock Exchange), but it was clearly increasing its market share of trading.

I called the state treasurer of Connecticut and outlined what was then an innovative tax-exempt bond financing structure that could attract the America Stock Exchange to Stamford. By then, the city was already benefiting from new first-class office buildings, particularly by the construction company of the hometown Rich Brothers.

The state's treasurer put me in touch with Attorney General Bob Killian, and we worked up a plan. Then we consulted with the Rich Brothers' organization and invited Mr. Levitt to Stamford for a presentation on moving to Stamford. I recall that we emphasized our plan was confidential, and that he explicitly agreed to the condition of keeping it confidential. We then outlined the proposal that the state would issue its general obligation bonds. The proceeds of those bonds would be expended to build a state-of-the-art home for housing the American Stock Exchange. It would either be its own building or a major tenant of a downtown Stamford office building. It would also be *basically rent free,* though the Exchange would be charged for standard services such as electricity, waste removal, and some maintenance expenses.

The key to the deal's structure was this: The state's financial experts had calculated the increased sales tax on the trading shares plus the number of expected bankers and staff who would be lured to live in Connecticut. Their state income taxes and the sales tax would more than cover the debt service on the state bonds, which would be issued at tax-exempt rates to build the facility.

At the time, using the state's general obligation tax exempt bond authority for such a purpose was novel. However, there were public purpose precedents for tax-exempt borrowing for public markets that I thought would support this modern-day exchange. Those of us presenting this plan believed we could persuade the American Stock Exchange to move to Stamford as its least costly option.

However, the move didn't happen because Mr. Levitt decided to "shop our proposal" despite such promise of confidentiality. When he returned to New York, within a short time, he called the Industrial Development Agency (IDA) of New York City. To the IDA officials, he outlined the plan we had presented and requested the Agency review the structure. After that, it could issue building bonds and lease free space to the Exchange in New York City.

The IDA responded that it would check with its bond counsel on the concept.

The irony, of course, was that my law firm partners represented the IDA and, naturally, I found out about this breach of confidentiality. Of course, we had no recourse and were not surprised when AMEX decided to stay in New York. I don't believe any of us at the Connecticut meeting ever received a formal response to our offer from Mr. Levitt, who went on to become chairman of the Securities and Exchange Commission.

CHAPTER 5

How New is Shady Tax Structuring?

The creation of the nonprofit New York Racing Association (NYRA) to own and manage Belmont, Aqueduct, and Saratoga horse racing tracks dates back to the 1950s. It was perhaps one of the best tax avoidance schemes for satisfying three constituencies: the wealthy, the public, and the governmental interests. This chapter describes its shady history and financial craftiness.

Horse racing and breeding has always been a major industry in New York State, and nothing compares to the festivities at Saratoga racetrack in the summer and the Triple Crown excitement of the Belmont Stakes. That's particularly true in years that a horse has already won both the Kentucky Derby and the Baltimore Preakness.

The third track in New York, Aqueduct, has lost some of its polish. Today, it combines harness and regular horse racing with casino activities.

In 1988, a friend and investment banker client, Gene Crowley, retained me. He invited me to dine at the elegant Solomon partners' dining room with fellow Yale graduate Dinny Phipps of Bessemer Trust.

Phipps had retained Solomon on behalf of the New York Racing Association (NYRA) to structure a financing deal that would help Belmont modernize its infrastructure. The question was how to develop a structure that could be financed with tax-exempt bonds.

While NYRA was a so-called tax-exempt charitable nonprofit, it could not under federal tax law issue the tax-exempt bonds; it would need legislation authorizing a conduit public authority to do so. To get to that conclusion, I had to research in depth exactly what NYRA was. It then became clear that special new state legislation would need to be carved especially for NYRA.

Even though Gene Crowley and I were seasoned in New York governmental finance, neither of us was prepared for what we learned as we walked the halls of Albany between the offices of certain legislators and the governor's staff.

Crafty Tax Structuring—Nothing New

Back in the 1950s, the Belmont family, the Phipps family, and the owners of the Aqueduct structured one of the most sophisticated tax shelters ever. They agreed to place each of their ownerships of the racetrack land in trust in a nonprofit corporation eventually known as the New York Racing Association (NYRA). That corporation would be devoted to a charitable purpose at its expiration in 2008. The charity would be designated by the governor of New York.[19]

By that arrangement, income from admission and other earnings of NYRA (a nonprofit) was exempt from state, city, and federal income taxes. Since there was a common ownership of the venues, the racing season for each could be scheduled in sequence and without concern about collusive antitrust noncompetitive allegations. That way, the establishment of blue blood families could compete with their horses and choice of trainers, jockeys, etc. In addition, the purses could be bigger due to the tax avoidance built into the NYRA structure.

In the 1980s, more than one thousand state employees were involved in overseeing the horse breeding and racing industry. The NYRA was considered a mythical entity akin to a secret society. The sheer number of state employees charged with regulating and supervising this industry made it seem like New York, in fact, was in charge of the racetrack business. At our meetings with the governmental assistants in Albany on a proposed tax-exempt bonding statute, we kept hearing they thought the state actually owned the tracks. We surmised that in attending for so many years to the oversight and regulation of the tracks, it seemed like the state was indeed the owner.

However, even with such oversight, NYRA had managed to have its share of adverse publicity on various bad practices. But every time the threat of a serious investigation to reorganize its governance arose, the NYRA would pull out an opinion written by Louis Lefkowitz, then a partner of the Nizer law firm and the state's venerable former attorney general.[20] He confirmed that NYRA did own the land of each venue; if need be, it could go out of the racing business altogether. It could even turn the beautiful historic grounds of both Saratoga and/or Belmont and/or Yonkers into housing developments.

Because of this ownership fact, the lobbying effort to restructure NYRA so it could be a tax-exempt issuer of bonds (like an Authority) became a non-starter.[21] NYRA leaders adamantly refused to tinker with its land titles, making it unfeasible to structure a secure tax-exempt bond issue. The fact that NYRA had a renewable franchise to operate and manage horse racing at the tracks was not considered property (like a lease) ownership interest. Therefore, bonds to finance improvements on its lands could not be secured by a mortgage or by net revenue pledges based on a "revocable" franchise.

Despite presenting several ways of recasting the structure, we finally had to give up on doing a bond financing in a tax-exempt way.

NYRA was considered a "bad manager" despite the blue bloods who were wonderful horse breeders and supportive of the industry. Mr. Phipps was a highly regarded advocate, but NYRA was just plain suspect of various corner-cutting (and guilty, as later investigations bore out). The law was even amended to require a legislative preapproval of the charity choice of the governor. NYRA finally gave up its ownership claims in return for (1) forgiveness of a series of money advances the state made for structural improvements to the tracks,[22] and (2) a state agreement with NYRA providing long-term franchise interests.

The economic benefits to New York from racing and horse breeding are enormous. However, the multiple levels and facets of the state's oversight suggest a seriously legitimate public perception that, unless carefully controlled, this industry was subject to scandal. Certainly, NYRA itself has had its share of notoriety. State oversight proved essential as NYRA experienced one scandal after another. Fortunately, there was never a perception that the actual races were fixed. Of course, today, the ownership of the tracks is in the title of the state. Accordingly, the tax exemption from federal, state, and city income taxes continues—and winning the purses remain the attraction for the owners. Simulcasting, online betting (without attendance at any track to place the bet), and casino activities are allowed, and the party goes on.

What revenues do the state and federal government receive? Tax payments on purse and ticket winnings and the income from the many employees at the tracks and at the horse breeding estates.

CHAPTER 6

How is Political Power Exercised?

The practice of bond counsel requires special education at a firm specializing in public finance. As a result, lawyers with that background are at a premium.

This chapter discusses the transfer of one expert attorney from the partnership of Hawkins Delafield to U.S. President Nixon's former law firm, Mudge Rose. It also explains the subsequent related move involving the legal work for financing multimillion-dollar construction costs for the transit system of the Washington Metropolitan Area Transit Authority ("Metro") from the Hawkins firm to President Nixon's former firm. (See Appendix A for related Washington Post *article.)*

For me, the major attraction of working at Hawkins in 1974 as an associate was that it had only fifteen partners and seven other associates—a ratio that appeared to make the path to partnership achievable. Within the Hawkins group were seven partners specializing in public finance. I soon learned that these partners had a veneer of gentility that masked their aggressive quest to gain control of clients.

Frank Wood, of the Wood group at Hawkins, controlled several major clients such as the Power Authority and the Triborough Bridge and Tunnel Authority. He had inherited these clients from Louis Delafield, who was Robert Moses's lawyer when those entities were chaired or created by New York and for which millions of bonds had been issued.

Below Wood were two other partners and a senior and a junior associate. Frank Curley, who styled himself as a new business lawyer, was next in tenure. Bob Ferdon, a brilliant working lawyer, was the third and youngest partner. Ike Russell, who headed another group, was the partner-in-charge of several of the firm's Turnpike Authorities, the Delaware Bridge Authority, and the Connecticut Expressway. He also managed the New Jersey public finance practice representing water and sewer authorities as well as many New Jersey towns, villages, and cities.

I was assigned to Gerard Fernandez, the partner who headed the New York general obligation practice. This group overlapped with the Wood group on new business. As a result, his contemporary, Curley, hardly spoke to Fernandez and actually fought over opening the morning mail. Often, potential bond clients sent in retainer requests to the firm without naming a particular partner, so whoever opened the letter also opened the file.

The Wood group, however, had moved in on Ike Russell's representation of the New Jersey Turnpike. Moreover, Bob Ferdon, the junior partner of the Wood group, had been asked to work with Ike on a major research project. That project consisted of plans for bonding the Washington DC Transit System, which would cross state borders into Virginia and Maryland and required a compact consented to by Congress under the U.S. Constitution. Remember, these were the days when loyalty to your firm was an unquestioned value, although claiming credit created controversy internally. Rewards were based on "finder, minder, and grinder" evaluations.

A Falling Out

In 1970, Frank Curley and Frank Wood had a falling out. While Fernandez was on vacation, Curley unilaterally moved a paralegal who worked for Fernandez to a new office a floor away from Fernandez. Wood ordered Curley to reinstate the paralegal to his original office, and Curley slammed Wood's door after the meeting. Shortly after, Curley left and became an investment banker at Dillon Read, an established blue blood Republican firm. Peter Flanigan of Dillon Read was a major supporter of Nixon's successful run for president in 1968.

Frank Curley, now at Dillon Read, made it known that the Washington Transit multibillion-dollar project was ready to have the funds released by the federal government to match the municipal bonding. He believed that Dillon Read should be the investment banker. President Nixon was also told by his staff that, as president of the United States, he controlled the release time. President Nixon wanted his former firm, Mudge Rose, to become the bond counsel. He particularly wanted to reward his former partner, current confidant, and campaign manager, John Mitchell.

Frank Curley made it known that, for it to be a smooth transition, the Mudge Rose firm needed to lure away Bob Ferdon from Hawkins. He argued that the complexities of the legal work would overwhelm the lawyers at Mudge, including Mitchell. And that's what happened.

One day, Bob Ferdon announced he and his senior associate were leaving Hawkins to both become partners at Mudge Rose. The next week, President Nixon released authorization for the financing. The foremost muckraker of the day, Jack Anderson, had the scoop, detailing the matter in two columns in the *Washington Post*. Ferdon's move was the first major move of a Wall Street partner from his established firm to another firm. It made headlines everywhere.[23]

The Hawkins firm moved quickly by recruiting Donald Robinson, Mitchell's then-associate, to move over to Hawkins from Mudge Rose as a partner. Robinson was totally miffed that Mitchell did not think he was lawyer enough to handle the DC matter. Those of us going through this experience were, naturally, not surprised at the later jailing of Mitchell as part of the Watergate cover-up.

The most ironic aspect is that John Mitchell had been the bond counsel for Nelson Rockefeller and was accustomed to counseling the politically powerful. He created certain special financing structures for Governor Rockefeller that continue today.

Mitchell's ethical lapses no doubt started when he poached Bob Ferdon from Hawkins, thereby breaking a long-standing tradition of Wall Street firms. Benefitting greatly from the Nixon/Mitchell connection, Ferdon successfully transferred other prestigious clients to Mudge Rose.[24]

To his credit, Wood maintained his stature in the firm and mentored Robinson for many years, including making him the managing partner. Years later, Robinson himself jumped ship to go to Orrick Herrington, taking several partners. This time, however, Hawkins was ready. On the day of Robinson's departure, someone delivered to Hawkins a list of Hawkins's clients that Robinson was likely to poach. An all-out effort by several Hawkins partners retained nine of the ten clients listed, including the Power Authority and other prestigious New York issuers.

CHAPTER 7

Officious Interference and Shady Claims

Eminent domain, sometimes called condemnation, refers to the power of the government under the 5th and 14th amendments of the U.S. Constitution to take private property for public use upon the payment of just compensation. Since the middle of the twentieth century, this power has been used by governments to redevelop economically depressed areas.

During the 1990s, New London, Connecticut, planned to have the Fort Turnbull neighborhood razed and rebuilt. After negotiating acceptable prices, 100 of 115 property owners voluntarily sold their properties. The remaining properties were condemned. In response, seven property owners sued in the Connecticut state courts and lost. They then appealed to the United States Supreme Court and lost again in 2005. Government officials in New London had obeyed all legal requirements, and the property had been properly condemned. But despite having lost in the highest court, the plaintiffs and their interloping lawyers refused to concede and continued to fight using public relations propaganda.

This chapter discusses how this case Kelo v. New London and subsequent nonsense has, to date, stymied the economic rejuvenation of the entire city to the detriment of resident taxpayers. As the recession and the effects of the court case recede, developers are showing renewed interest in returning this property to the tax rolls.

For practicing lawyers, nothing is more professional than dealing with matters of serious national public policy that require the Supreme Court of the United States (SCOTUS) to establish the validity of an option you've counseled a client to take. Frankly, nothing is more tension-filled than having a case accepted by SCOTUS (or a state's highest court) that litigates an option you've already counseled and your client has taken. If your advice has been wrong, this puts the client materially at risk.

Shades of Public Finance, Volume 1, includes several chapters featuring successful results in cases like this. Chapter 11 in this Volume 2 details a Tenth Amendment case that restored the rule of law by holding that states have the constitutional sovereign right to preclude from federal taxation the interest on their bonds issued for public purposes. This chapter discusses my experience serving (as a voluntary advisor) on one of the most publicized, criticized, and, in my view, wasteful episodes that, unfortunately until now, has prevented New London from a near-magical economic development achievement.

The Holdouts and Their Supporters

The Institute of Justice, a self-described "nonprofit libertarian public interest law firm,"[25] was working with University of Chicago Professor

Richard Epstein[26] (now emeritus), also a self-described personal rights libertarian. Displaying their skepticism of authority and state power, they both injected themselves into New London's "eminent domain" economic development procedures by latching on to several holdouts —clients who challenged the "taking" of their homes. SCOTUS, in *Kelo v. City of New London*,[27] ruled in favor of New London. Unequivocally, the city had held its process and determinations within the parameter of established law.

In 1954, SCOTUS established in Berman v. Parker the requirements for a government condemnation to further economic redevelopment.[28] In *Kelo*, it relied on and reaffirmed Berman, stating again that the government can transfer property from one private party to another as long as just compensation is provided, the redevelopment pursuant to which the transfer is planned serves a public purpose, and the government procedures have met due process and public notice requirements. In *Berman*, the owners of a thriving department store had their property condemned as part of a Washington, DC, plan to redevelop a large area afflicted with urban blight. Despite the owners' best efforts to resist, Berman's department store was legally torn down and the area redeveloped.[29]

In New London, despite the city's following due process and the established law (as both the State Supreme Court and SCOTUS held), the Institute of Justice and Professor Epstein drummed up publicity to portray city leaders and the Pfizer Corporation as institutions stealing the home of one Ms. Kelo. They did not refer to established legal precedents and the Fifth and Fourteenth constitutional amendments that authorize this kind of taking or challenge that the redevelopment plan or the required determinations were arbitrary or capricious. Nor did they acknowledge the huge potential benefits to the taxpayers of New London that would result from this eminent domain condemnation. Finally, at no time did those out-of-state lawyers understand

and balance their rhetoric to acknowledge the overall state policy to enhance its distressed cities. The Institute for Justice has been properly criticized by Timothy Hollister, an outstanding real estate lawyer and partner in a prestigious Connecticut law firm, for missing (or purposely missing) what the lawyer believes would have been winning arguments. This is based on Connecticut law decisions that had narrowed federal case law. By winning, the lawyer means that Ms. Kelo would have been able to remain in her home because, under those state cases, the NLDC could not have proved the "necessity" of taking her house to achieve the basic development. That learned Connecticut lawyer suggests that, in their zeal to achieve its national libertarian agenda, a winning decision on local law was of no value. Moreover, according to his analysis of both decisions in the state and federal Supreme Courts, the justices wondered why the state law issue was not litigated.[30]

The most sophisticated and smartest analysis of the current reforms that certain states have or have not enacted was the subject of a professor's testimony at a federal hearing on proposed federal legislation to override the *Kelo* case upholding economic development takings.[31] Professor John A. Echeverria persuasively testified that narrowing the national standard reaffirmed by the *Kelo* case would be the wrong Federal policy because most states have debated the issue and make policy decisions best for jurisdictions This outcome reflects the best in our democratic process and sovereign states system.

The worst public deception, however, was conducted by *The New London Day,* the venerable newspaper of record for the city. Despite repeated efforts by city leaders to educate the editor and lead columnists, its headlines and editorials repeatedly sided with the holdout owners. The paper offered little reporting on the huge economic benefit from increased taxes and employment expected from completing the condemnation in a timely fashion. It conducted no investigation or research to educate their readers on the reason "eminent domain" exists as an absolute government power. And not once could I find mention of that leading precedent, the *Berman v. Parker* case, in *The Day.* It is documented that the publisher of the paper ended a meeting to persuade him to back the project by admitting he was a libertarian, that he was personally against the government's effort, and that his paper would remain in opposition to it.[32]

Suffered Economic Decline; Declared a Distressed City

Over several decades, New London had slowly suffered economic decline. Those who governed the state of Connecticut, moreover, had designated New London as being distressed under a statute that extended state aid and power to take remedial action.[33] In addition, the U.S. Navy closed the Undersea Warfare Center in 1996. From the 1940s, the Center had been curtained off from the rest of the Fort Trumbull area by no trespassing signs and threatening barbed-wired fencing. The closure resulted in more than a thousand local jobs lost.

The Fort Trumbull neighborhood was isolated from Pequot Avenue—the main road leading to the beaches—by Amtrak's railroad bridges. It was also home to a smelly city wastewater treatment plant as well as scrap metal and boat repair junkyards. Sailors seeking and those offering fun often loitered here. Significant numbers of both commercial and residential building were either vacant, under short-term rentals, and in poor to below-average condition.

In 1998, the Pfizer Corporation announced it would build a large research facility on a Pequot Avenue site backing on the Long Island Sound near the fort. The state had authorized significant bond issue dollars to restore the Fort Trumbull site to a public park facility and to fund the environmental clean up cost of the contaminated junk yard site.

In anticipation, the city had formed the New London Development Corporation (NLDC) to plan for redeveloping the 90 acres in the Fort Trumbull neighborhood. Of the 115 property owners there, 100 voluntarily sold their property to the NLDC. Seven owners who owned the remaining fifteen properties refused. The city and NLDC condemned these properties while offering fair value. As noted earlier, the property owners sued and, after losing in the highest Connecticut state court, appealed to the United State Supreme Court, where they again lost.

Governor Rell's Contradictory Action

Subsequent to and despite the detailed, well-written opinion of the SCOTUS in the Kelo case, sympathy for Ms. Kelo's losing her home increased due to the inflammatory but dissenting opinion of Justice Sandra Day O'Connor. Added to that was the highly publicized griping by the Institute for Justice and Professor Epstein. This prompted the then-governor of Connecticut, Jodi Rell, to counter the decision of Rear Admiral (Ret.) David Goebel, executive director of NLDC, and ordered the board to have him rescind the eviction notices that had been mailed to the holdouts after they lost the case.

Governor Rell's surprising command contradicted the statutory state policy, the state's prior financial support of this project, past coordination of activity, and the gubernatorial-controlled state bond commission bond appropriations. This dictate was likely prompted by her political prospects in the upcoming election. It took a special controversial advisory opinion of the state's elected attorney general (after his review of the "private emoluments" gift prohibition in the state constitution) for the NLDC to execute the governor's dictate to the board. That meant both forgiving the considerable amount of back rent and taxes owed by the holdouts and increasing the "fair value" amount to be paid to them.

Resignations of certain board members because of such political interference and termination of staff resulting from political orders followed. The momentum to rebuild dissipated. The governor's intrusion caused even more delay and I believe would not have happened if Governor Rowland, a huge supporter of city development, had remained in office. The only major newspaper support for SCOTUS's *Kelo* decision came from the editors of *The New York Times.* (See Appendix B.) They agreed that the cities of America need to use the principle of eminent domain (as exercised by NLDC) for their economic development.

A Martyr

The Institute of Justice no doubt in my view told Ms. Kelo of the higher payments awarded to the last holdout in these cases as an incentive to let the Institute take over her defense. I do not know whether the Institute or Professor Epstein was paid directly by a share of Ms. Kelo's award (or indirectly as a charitable gift of hers) or whether the Institute's remuneration comes from tax deductible payments to the Institute or whether it received any remuneration at all, as the publicity of its role was, intrinsically probably worthwhile. The intellectual challenge to be in the game, I imagine, might have worked well enough for the professor.

As it happened, the Institute's tactics provided an absolute win-win for Ms. Kelo because, when she lost her case, she bought a waterfront home out of town and became a martyr for the sake of homeowners everywhere. In that role, she made lots of media appearances as the victim staving off the big bad wolf of governments.[34]

The Distress Designation and the Timeline

What was my involvement in the *Kelo* case? Let me provide some background.

Richard Schneller was the majority leader of the Connecticut state senate when I met him. He was a successful businessman from Essex, Connecticut, who had a wonderful long-term friendship with Governor William O'Neill, one of the nation's best Irish-American politicians. O'Neill had made it possible for Dick to be the chair of the influential senate legislature's State and Urban Development Committee.

On behalf of the state treasurer, I had been asked to draft and testify before that committee on legislation allowing towns and cities to pursue economic development including use of eminent domain and municipal bond financing. This would particularly apply in cities that had been already designated distressed and had fallen further behind when urban shopping centers and corporate headquarters pursued pristine opportunities in the green Connecticut suburbs.[35]

This trend started in the 1960s. An example is Bloomfield, just outside of Hartford (once known as the insurance capital city of the nation), where a major insurance company built a fabulous corporate campus. It left one of its competitors stuck in downtown Hartford with its congested traffic issues. In Rocky Hill, the state built an opulent building on a hill to house its expanding Department of Transportation. The state's major utility, Northwest Utilities, located its New England headquarters on a neighboring hill. Both were near Route 15, which allowed commuters easy access without contending with inner city traffic.

During this period, the continuing deterioration of Connecticut cities became a matter of great concern for the state. Bridgeport and Waterbury had staved off bankruptcy; only Stamford was luring businesses out of New York City and seemed sound. Barely fiscally stable were New Haven and Hartford, with Yale University and the state capital as anchors, respectively.[36] In the New London case, the state supported its policy with a substantial amount of state bond financing.[37]

After I testified before his committee, Dick suggested I talk to Claire Gaudiani,[38] president of Connecticut College. Its campus was up on a hill and across from the Coast Guard Academy in New London. Dick was a member of the Board of Trustees. Hawkins, my firm, had already been designated by the state financing authority to be bond counsel on new buildings for Connecticut College.

Shortly after, Dick visited me at my summer home in New London and realized my passion for that city. We agreed it was unfortunate that superhighway I-95 had separated its downtown from the campuses of both Connecticut College and the Coast Guard Academy. In effect, it had isolated those two institutions of learning. To overcome this separation, Claire's vision was to permit her students to have an urban experience during their student years, so she located some of the classrooms on State Street, the main street, with several vacant store fronts. By then, high-end retail clothing and sports stores had relocated to the massive shopping mall in suburban Waterford off I-95.[39]

At the time we met, Claire was involved in one of the most important events ever to happen to an impoverished city. She had persuaded George Milne, then head of Pfizer Corporation, to locate a needed new building in New London, directly across the river from its vast manufacturing facilities in Groton. There would be delightful boat rides ferrying employees between the two sites. This would be his global research headquarters for proving the commercial viability of certain proposed drugs. By doing this, she was advocating a pincer attack to reestablish New London with vibrant city life and an educated work force. The college would come down from the hill, becoming a major activity center for students, teachers, and stores on State Street and bars and restaurants on Bank Street. Down the road to the left of Bank Street, Pfizer, fronting on Pequot Avenue, would have a magnificent building. It would employ thousands of young scientists to work there and maybe live in the city.

Claire was so enthusiastic and optimistic about this concept that she persuaded her board to invest in three old but restorable-to-residential classic New England business buildings on State Street. She knew that some of her students would prefer urban living to dormitory life and, with the young Pfizer professionals, they would live in refurbished apartments and enjoy downtown. The scientists would be able to easily walk to the Pfizer facility. Activity on State and Bank streets would feature local artists' renderings, coffee lattes, and more.

To summarize, Pfizer built its global research center on Pequot Avenue, including a prominent and attractive day care center across the street so working parents could visit their children at lunch. Connecticut College bought the three buildings to re-engineer for residential use and also planned to rent space on State Street for classrooms. Eventually, though, the college's faculty balked about teaching downtown. After that, the city council refused to bond $10 million as its local share of the restorations, after which would have followed a substantial state grant.

NLDC

Concerning the Pfizer move, Claire's official role was as head of the new NLDC.[40] The city's urban renewal agency had been riddled with rumors of political patronages, graft, and greed; it was clearly not deserving of carrying out the state's clean-up contamination contracts for the Fort Trumbull site. Jay Levin, a local attorney and former mayor of New London, had a retainer from NLDC to work out the local politics with the city council. The project was turned over to the new NLDC, installing Claire Gaudiani as its president. (It helped that Jay was an alumni of Connecticut College.) Jay also had another NLDC retainer lobbying for the state's appropriations for both the restoration of Fort Trumbull and removal of the scrapyard contaminants. Best of all, David Goebel, a former commander of a Navy submarine who had retired in New London, was hired to be NLDC's executive director.

The Coast Guard Academy has a beautiful campus in New London, backing on the Thames River. Across the river in Groton is the U.S. Navy's submarine base and one of the two American plants that manufactures nuclear submarines. (General Dynamics had acquired the Electric Boat Company and constructed at least one submarine a year at a guarded facility on the Thames River next to the main Groton Pfizer buildings.[41])

To summarize, the institutional leadership of the city of New London had come together in coordinating this historic and huge renewal in a community that had fallen on hard times. It was once primed to put into effect the state of Connecticut's pronounced on-going policy to reestablish the economic viability of its major cities. As the state's flagship enterprise, the University of Connecticut established branches in downtown Stamford, Waterbury, and Hartford. State officials were also looking for ways to help New London.

What would complete this restoration? Developing the so-called Fort Trumbull site next to the Pfizer building. Both of them backed on the entrance to the Thames River from Long Island Sound, and no more beautiful views could be found anywhere. This area was completely cut off from the rest of the summer traffic as well as the high-priced residential homes fronting on Pequot Avenue and the entrance to the New London Harbor by the Amtrak railroad bridges (literally, on the "other side" of the tracks).

Besides attracting fun seeking sailors from the submarine base, it was the site of a smelly sewage treatment plant, a scrap and metal junkyard, a private club, open ship or furniture repair yards and motely buildings, and one- or two-level housing with small lawns or no lawns. Some of the homes were frequently rented out; others were modest family homes. None were on the water, and a very few had a view of the water that was mostly blocked by the Fort and Navy buildings.

The NLDC had received a written proposal from a major hotel developer selected in a competitive bidding process. It was attracted not only by this water view site but also by the clear commercial advantage of being, by proximity alone, the preferred accommodation for professional visitors who would consult with the new research center's scientists.

For the record, I can state that the Pfizer decision to build its global research center on the New London side was never legally contingent on developing the surrounding area. George Milne of Pfizer was on the board of the NLDC for a while,[42] thus he consulted regularly with state and city leaders. But at no time were the actions of the NLDC dictated or even demanded by Pfizer.[43] It simply made the most commercial and economic sense for NLDC to pursue hotel and other core businesses to take advantage of being next to such a sophisticated business with well-educated employees. Also, Claire had a clear vision of the symmetry of this Fort Trumbull area activity and downtown New London; and she seemed to have consolidated power to make it happen.

The rest, as they say, is history. The Institute stopped site development using litigation and publicity tactics that turned the tide of opinion against this project. It unfairly victimized both Pfizer as the villain, and Goebel and Gaudiani as henchmen hijacking the home of a little old lady. (Ms. Kelo had allegedly already applied for a mortgage to buy a new home and claimed it would be her primary residence when the Institute of Justice came knocking.) Due to the litigation delay and Governor Rell's actions that stopped taking properties from the few holdouts (leading to increased payouts for their property), the city's taxpayers lost the substantial tax base that a hotel and other businesses would have provided. This loss of revenue and increased expenditure became a double whammy to these taxpayers.[44]

The Cost of Delay

Why did this delay matter so much? There are two sad but simple answers. First, a recession in the national economy changed the dynamics of doing business. As a result, the bank refused to renew its mortgage financing commitment to the hotel developer. The bank, the developer, and other businesses had lost enthusiasm due to the black-eye punch of the Institute of Justice's negative publicity about a Fort Trumbull address.

Second, and most critical, is that during the period of delay, Pfizer had completed a merger with another major drug company.[45] The redundancy of two large research facilities and staff required not only abandoning its new corporate research headquarters in New London but also shutting down several buildings in Groton,[46] even razing one to lower the tax value of the property.[47]

What's Happening Today?

New London and the state quickly enlisted General Dynamics (apparently with significant tax abatement benefits) to move into the abandoned Pfizer building. However, the day care center activity was not continued, leaving that facility vacant so far. General Dynamics is expanding and hiring New London residents to meet its needs. The NLDC has changed its name. Claire Gaudiani writes books on philanthropy, consults, and lives in New York, having left after thirteen years as president of Connecticut College. The buildings the college bought never became the homes of those young students or scientists. David Goebel stands tall as he walks along his home street fronting on the beaches off of Pequot Avenue, the very road Eugene O'Neill lived on. The author had described the road in *Long Day's*

Journey Into the Night as usually camouflaged by the fog coming off Long Island Sound. Goebel wonders what could have been—and what still may happen.

As both the recession and the *Kelo* wave recede, there is evidence of renewed interest by developers and the return of this property to the tax rolls.[48] Fortunately, General Dynamics has taken full occupancy of the magnificent modern building with windows and walking views of Long Island Sound. The renamed development authority is entertaining a renewed interest by developers of the neighboring site. The city, its residents, and its visitors are enjoying a stunning waterfront park and the renovated Fort Trumbull, with regular outdoor performances by the Coast Guard Band. The site has been completely cleared and become a welcome resting place for migratory birds. This area has given the city a chance to compete with neighboring suburbs for economic development as the market revives.

New London, once a highly prosperous whaling city, still struggles economically. The protestors—in their zealous, unsuccessful effort—were prevented from changing the law. However, if the urban development had occurred when all the stars of prosperity were aligned, it would have been a major service to the residents of the town and their tax base much earlier.[49]

Further Analyses

Lest we leave this chapter only hanging on to the hope of the Fort Trumbull site being finally developed, the intervention by the Institute of Justice needs critical analysis.

"The substantive result of *Kelo v. New London* is neither surprising nor novel."[50] SCOTUS confirmed there was no litmus "metric for economic development such as a blight requirement"[51] under the U.S. constitutional power. Accordingly, I question the propriety of the Institute of Justice's tax-exempt nonprofit status as it pursued a political agenda of so-called libertarianism devoid of a charitable or other qualifying tax-exempt status. Moreover, the Institute failed to develop an argument that it would have not only benefited the holdouts but the other property owners while advancing its agenda as well.

Here is why: In Chapter 10, Volume 1, I discussed why the Patriots professional football team did not move to Hartford, Connecticut. The site of a proposed new stadium was identified for development by the chairman of Phoenix Insurance Company long before the state or that company had secured ownership or even the right to buy the parcels. The fair value of those parcels to be established in a state condemnation was greatly enhanced by the announced state plan to build a stadium on the site.

Why did the Institute not claim a percentage of the anticipated tax roll huge increase as just compensation for the Fort Trumbull site property owners by the announced plan to have a prestigious hotel and modern office buildings built? That option would have been an honorable way of intruding. After all, in my opinion, it was a foregone legal and correct conclusion based on the prior decisions of SCOTUS, that Ms. Kelo would lose the right to remain in her house. If she and the other holdouts had left at the date of "taking," then a hotel and new office buildings would be on the tax rolls today. In fact, the holdouts could probably have negotiated a larger just compensation award than what resulted from the Institute's heavy handed tactics.[52]

For clarity, the concept is this: If future use of a site by the proposed plan is the basis of determining fair compensation, then the owners of land being condemned would be entitled to the percentage of that according to their percent of the whole site valuation as developed in accordance with the plan. That would discourage a lot of takings, but it might be the correct analysis of fair compensation.

Currently, there is confusion about how to properly determine fair value. Historically, it has been based on *current* zoning, services, and uses rather than *anticipated* renewal use and services not yet built. However, for estate taxes, a lot of farmland is being valued according to highest and best use of that land. It has become the basis for determining the value when states buy the "development rights" to permit heirs to continue farming. (See Chapter 14, Volume 1, *Shades of Public Finance,* for discussion of the first state program and its progeny in many other communities.)

These considerations could have played a much larger role in the *Kelo* case.

Part Three

Overview of Municipal Law

CHAPTER 8

Why a Public Authority?

This chapter answers the question about the value of setting up a public authority based on my experience with the state of Connecticut as an example.

Every state has come to the twenty-first century with an assortment of embedded financial structures[53] initially developed during the 1920 to 1950 period.[54] They've accelerated tremendously from the 1970s forward, primarily as a result of citizens' increased demand for state and local government to finance infrastructure. This includes housing for low- and moderate-income families, sewage treatment plants to eliminate septic tanks as the suburbs expanded, local water treatment facilities, and pollution control loan programs. Add to that the major expansion of all kinds of transportation infrastructure including toll turnpikes, bridges, airports, transit facilities, commuter railroads, and even bike paths.

The remarkable expansion of public financing purposes has sparked the development of financial structuring of bond programs and a multibillion-dollar tax-exempt public finance industry of lawyers, investment bankers, feasibility consultants, engineers, architects, and financial advisors. Probably the first major expansion in New York was under Nelson Rockefeller, who established the New York Housing

Finance Agency (discussed later in this chapter). It was created to finance and build large-scale clustered buildings or "projects" to house low-income residents.

In the early 1940s, Connecticut Governor Chester Bowles's program established an authorization of a general obligation of bonds of $120 million (in today's dollar approximately $3 billion). They were secured for bond market purposes by the general credit or general fund of the state government but proclaimed to be self-supporting. This was due to a series of loans made to local housing authorities in each of its major cities to build, own, operate, and maintain projects using rental income from the tenants.

Today, the downside of living in "projects" is well-known, but every city in Connecticut still has legacy housing from the Bowles's program. Exceptions exist elsewhere such as Stuyvesant housing in Manhattan, but in Connecticut, I'm not familiar with any legacy housing of the Bowles's program that has thrived. Most are either being torn down or slowly rehabilitated; the majority badly need repair and maintenance.[55]

Connecticut Mortgage Authority

In 1972, I received a call from Connecticut Commissioner of Revenue George Conkling, the financial genius and long-serving civil servant who kept Connecticut's general fund balanced. Because of him, the state stayed first in state fiscal categories for many years.

He called about my reviewing a draft prepared by Ed Marcus, head of the Connecticut Democratic Party. The draft legislation would create the Connecticut Mortgage Authority (CMA). In many respects, it would replicate the New York Housing Finance Authority (HFA) so Connecticut could finance developers in constructing housing for low- and moderate-income families. (See Appendix D for details on what happened in New York state.)

Connecticut's constitution does not have a referendum requirement as New York does. The only constitutional provision restricting debt incurrence is that no one could spend taxpayers' dollars unless those funds were used for a public purpose. But that restriction became meaningless given that the judicial decisions determining public purpose are deferred to the Connecticut's state legislature.

I counseled George Conkling that Connecticut did not need to create an authority as New York did. Why? If the state wanted to restrict the use of the general credit or general fund, the state could structure the debt as a state revenue bond comparable to the bond structure my mentor at Hawkins, Ike Russell, had devised. Russell used the structure to finance the Greenwich-Killingly Expressway (later called I-95 Expressway) Revenue Bonds issued by a committee under the state of Connecticut's name. At the time of that financing, Conkling was the commissioner of transportation under Governor Abe Ribicoff and helped structure those state revenue bonds.

Conkling then instructed me that the state of Connecticut would *not* issue housing bonds under its name, whether general obligation or revenue bonds. From the Bowles program, he'd learned that those housing authorities had defaulted on their loans because they knew the state would pay the debt service on the bonds to avoid a bond default. He was convinced it wouldn't matter if the bonds were revenue bonds or general obligation bonds of the state. If the state's name was on the bonds, the result would be the same. But he indicated he had no policy objection to creating a state authority with a board made up of the State Bond Commission or its appointees (excluding the attorney general, whose office he considered overburdened).

Then I asked permission to research a kind of state credit enhancement. Conkling gave me a green light, particularly if I could build in a year's reserve fund to delay the need to appropriate the necessary funds. He wanted to create a separate authority to manage the revenue bond program and enforce the payment of rents but not as a means to circumvent a referendum or other constitutional requirement. Not surprisingly, that same motivation of managing projects—especially those entailing political risk such as displacing residents to allow the Cross Bronx Expressway—had motivated Robert Moses to favor the public authority financing structure.[56]

Solution Based on Nineteenth-Century Precedent

After considerable research, I came up with a unique enhancement structure based directly on Connecticut law, albeit a fairly old law. During the 1800s, the Connecticut legislature met only in even years. Its members dealt with unexpected spending authorizations by approving the concept of "deemed to be appropriated." This way, they could authorize the executive branch to spend money for unexpected cost increases over budget during the odd year without convening a special session. From that, I concluded that in Connecticut, it could be set up as a mandatory "fill up" rather than a moral obligation, based on this precedent.

The draft of the Special Capital Reserve Fund (SCRF) enhancement provided that the Authority deposit from each bond issue proceeds an amount of the maximum of debt service in any year the bonds are to be outstanding. If, in any year thereafter, it became necessary to draw on the reserve to pay debt service, then the state treasurer must deposit that amount in the SCRF from the general fund. The amount was, by statute, "deemed to be appropriated" for that purpose. Unlike New York, this structure creates a legal state guarantee without concern of violating any debt referendum restriction.

This enhancement was accepted by the marketplace. Our opinion stated that the "amount certified as necessary to fill the reserve" was "validly deemed appropriated" and therefore the state treasurer would be required to deposit such an amount from the general fund. Because the bonds were not direct faith and credit debt of the state, the rating agencies gave a rating one notch below the state bonds rating to the Connecticut Housing Finance Authority.

However, I was concerned that such a strong state security support could still leave state coffers at risk. So I drafted strong language requiring the board to authorize each bond issue to determine that, after a careful review of the loans to be made with the proceeds, the revenues from them were expected to be sufficient to pay debt service. That meant the feasibility or self-sufficiency of the loan documents and resources of the developers was a statutory determination that must be recorded. If the documents weren't recorded, the bonds could not be issued upon the reliance of SCRF "fill up."

The concept of requiring a formal declaration of self-sufficiency proved to be prescient. Please review the details in Appendix D respecting New York's experience with "moral obligation" bonds. In that situation, a self-sufficient financing declaration was not statutorily required.

General Bond Resolution

The other valuable feature I drafted for Connecticut was the General Bond Resolution. It combined financing all projects' in a single document financing rather than doing what New York's HFA did, which was one bond resolution for each project. The economics of scale, cross calls, arbitrage benefits, regularity of large offerings, and common SCRF security provision proved enormously important as the program grew in size to exceed $3 billion. Today, it is considered the best bond of all state HFAs.

Connecticut recognized the benefit of creating public authorities for special financing for which there was a revenue resource other than the state's taxing power. It also valued driving down the interest cost by adding the SCRF as long as each board of the authority made a self-sufficiency determination. I was retained to include that credit enhancement for the Connecticut Development Authority to reduce the interest rate for small manufacturing plant loans, for the Connecticut Resource Recovery Authority to finance certain waste-to-energy resource recovery plants, for the University of Connecticut to finance residential and parking facilities at the Storrs campus, and for certain types of educational facilities.

Triple-A Ratings

The most interesting benefit from the SCRF derived from years of doing refundings on a current-year basis. It finally dawned on me that having this one-year reserve in trust to pay the year's debt service meant the bonds maturing that year were entitled to be rated triple A.

After years of coaxing the rating agencies, I finally succeeded in persuading them that any bond enhanced by a SCRF should be rated the same as the state's bonds. Why? First, because the mandatory "fill up" was at least as secure as a "faith and credit" obligation to pay debt service on a general obligation state bond. Second, the state didn't require a referendum to incur debt, so it would not be inappropriate or illegal to consider it the equivalent of debt.

I asked the agencies to view the SCRF like a secure escrow fund of that year's debt service, triple-A funds on hand, and an obligation of the state to "fill up" as strong as a state appropriation of debt service. That did it! All bonds secured by a SCRF were upgraded. This astonished the state treasurer, Denise Nappier, who had not asked me to take on this assignment.

To this day, I'm not sure she thought it was a good idea. It meant bonds of the authorities that had the SCRF enhancement were rated the same as the state's bonds and therefore competed with them.

CHAPTER 9

What Is a Second Injury Fund?

This chapter explains the history of the Second Injury Fund and my role in creating a financing program for Connecticut and New York to bail out mismanagement in both states.

From 1975 through 2005, I had either prime responsibility or co-responsibility for the due diligence and disclosure of the bond offering statements of the state of Connecticut. I also conducted formal due diligence sessions with state officials to be sure all important financial matters were properly disclosed. (See Chapter 12 in this book for the story of disclosure requirements for municipal offerings.)

For the offering document the state would certify a negative assurance opinion is rendered stating that all material matters are included, and no material matters are excluded. Despite this diligence, the state of Connecticut (among others) had a long-standing financing program "hidden" in plain view under the category of workmen's compensation.

Second Injury Fund

In 1995, Connecticut's treasurer, Denise Nappier, retained me to review the law and financing history of the state's second injury fund. What is a second injury fund? When men (mostly) came home from WWII with a so-called first injury (e.g., losing an arm), the chances of them being hired was poor. This was because if any of these people lost the other arm on the job, the employer's insurance company would be subject to a workman's compensation liability, likely paying out for the employee's entire life. As a result, employers were *not* hiring veterans who had a first injury.

Connecticut's Experience

The state of Connecticut addressed this issue by passing legislation to require that first injury job applicants not be subject to discrimination because of that injury. The law authorized the employer to transfer his account over to the state's Second Injury Fund upon a second injury to that employee. Rather than the employer carrying the continued workman's compensation liability, the state assumed that responsibility.[57]

The annual accumulated charges under the Second Injury Fund were assessed to all employers in the state. That meant, by law, no employer could discriminate and reject a job applicant because of a first injury. This straightforward solid public purpose came about well before the Americans with Disabilities Act (ADA) was passed in 1990. Initially, it appeared to work well by helping employ soldiers who had suffered injuries in combat.

But over time, the number of second injury cases increased as the program continued. Before long, it included Korean and Vietnamese war veterans. It also grew to include any worker with a first injury regardless of military service.

Surprisingly, during all these years of due diligence discussing debt, budget, and financial developments, I had never heard of or read about a Second Injury Fund. That's because it was treated differently than the general fund or highway fund or other programs requiring legislative appropriations. The state's treasurer had sole authority to assess employers in the state for the payments due the beneficiaries of the fund. Accordingly, it was not supported or thought of as funded by taxes, and it wasn't included in the budget proposed by the governor and approved by the legislature. The state auditors and independent accountants did not consider it a general fund asset or liability; it was presented and accounted for under "trust funds."

A Mandated Charge

In the reality of the federal, state, and tax law, however, the assessment on employers was a mandated charge equivalent to a corporate tax. In effect, it was a disguised "cost of doing corporate business" in Connecticut. My review clarified that the state was not even managing the fund as an insurer would. The state simply started paying the injured employee (including medical needs) and assessing all employers once the claim was transferred to the Second Injury Fund.

I was retained when the assessment was being adjusted to quarterly from annually because the number of claims along with the attendant costs had escalated. Unlike practices in private insurance companies (ironically, Connecticut is known for that industry), the state never managed this responsibility as a private insurer would. For example, the state did not initiate efforts to provide rehabilitation after the second injury. Also, it did not maintain active tracking of the post -injury activities of the recipients. (Think welfare checks without recurring investigations of work impairment.)

At the urging of the state treasurer, the attorney general's office investigated the lifestyles of those "permanently disabled" second injured receiving checks from the state. It found many lived in Florida (or Connecticut) doing "off book" work. The treasurer focused on this issue after state auditors publicly warned that the unfunded accrued liability had increased to about $15 billion. The auditors also said the assessments were covering only the annual amount payable without any backup reserve for the balance accruing in succeeding years. The treasurer led the effort to pass legislation and close the program to new entries, which was done. The statute also authorized tax-exempt bonds to finance lump sum settlements to be negotiated with beneficiaries rather than annual lifetime monthly checks.

When the Americans for Disabilities Act was passed in 1990, it precluded this kind of hiring discrimination, which meant there was no longer a need for the state program. In fact, it should have been closed at the time that federal legislation was passed.

Adopted by Other States

Meanwhile, almost every state had adopted a similar program with similar experiences as Connecticut. Ironically, the publicity of the Connecticut public bond offering to fund the lump sum payments attracted attention everywhere. As a result, several other states noticed a considerable jump in applicants.

Working in one state on innovative financing often presented opportunities in another state for new legal business. Also, the practice required me to review the laws of the other states for precedents. So I was surprised a year later to be called by David English, the senior budget officer for the state of New York, about doing similar second injury financing. (I'd previously worked with Dave on state budget and bonding issues.)

My first reaction was to tell him I had previously checked and had not found such a second injury fund in New York. English replied that it was called the Special Liability Fund and could be found in the statutory book called "Miscellaneous," not the "State Finance" book. As it was, in Connecticut, it was hiding in plain sight (which is why I had not found it). Not only was the unfunded accrued liability in excess of $20 billion, but New York had been a first in the nation applying the state umbrella insurance fund to first injury veterans returning from World War I.

Interestingly, the huge jump in New York in the qualified beneficiaries transferred to the fund in that year was directly related to the publicity of the Connecticut deal in the marketplace. This indicated that some smart financial folks, noticing the Connecticut deal, were advising New York companies providing workman's compensation insurance and making them aware of a similar New York program. Accordingly, these companies shifted many of their former employees with second injuries over to the Special Liability Fund of New York.

New York's Experience

David English shepherded legislation (drafted similar to Connecticut's) through passage in New York. This closed the fund to new second injury cases and authorized the financing of lump sum settlements with existing beneficiaries. He also determined the first effort in reducing this liability would be an all-out effort to "sell" the whole portfolio to an insurance company by *paying* an experienced claims management insurer. The financing would be for the state to issue bonds to pay an insurer and allow that insurer to create a huge fund for investment. This would produce sufficient revenues to pay the annual amounts due to the recipients, including medical costs.

I explained that the state treasurer in Connecticut had undertaken a similar effort but concluded it was impractical. In effect, the portfolio was so complicated that making a reasonable "valuation" was almost impossible. In Connecticut, since the staff at the treasurer's office knew the most about the portfolio, that "staff" could form its own company to bid or be hired intact by an insurance bidder. However, this was fraught with potential adverse publicity about the portfolio, so the treasurer decided not to pursue the idea.

English then hired a nationally recognized firm, Milliman & Co., to develop the protocol for qualifying bidders. We went to work on a potential bond issue that would finance the payment to the company that was asked to bid a fixed dollar amount—without any exceptions, contingences, or rejects. Because of that, the company would "assume" the liability of the special fund—a lump sum settlement of the entire liability.

The portfolio was subject to certain confidentiality protocols. It was also subject to review by several well-known substantial insurance companies. But despite many due diligence sessions to develop the characteristics of the million recipients, there seemed to be no reasonable way to understand future costs that would be incurred for both the medical and compensation payments. This program had been "unmanaged" by the state for so many years, none of the statistical data regarding life expectancy understood by the insurance companies could be applied.

The concept of "low hanging fruit" (meaning some were easy to calculate but others were tricky and didn't "hang low") meant any bids would necessarily include the conditions of not accepting or returning to the state those cases that were too "costly." In the end, like Connecticut, New York's effort to offload the whole liability of the fund failed. Instead, a smaller bond issue went forward to anticipate an estimated number of "lump sum settlements" that recipients would agree to receive.

Yet even that task proved to be costly and fraught with issues. For example, what is the state's risk if a recipient of the lump settlement sum takes the cash and loses it all at Connecticut casinos? Does that person not fall back on the welfare of the state?

For bond issues to qualify as tax-exempt, payment of the settlement must be an arm's- length settlement of a liability (like the bonding of a judgment). State laws could not restrict how the recipients invested or spent the money received. This meant only payment of "lump sum settlements" qualified the bond issue as tax-exempt. Any bond issue that only "funded" the current liability would be treated the same as a pension fund and be considered a taxable arbitrage bond.

Basic Lesson Learned

What was the basic lesson learned from this program? That the public policy at the time of creation was important to encourage employers to hire injured war veterans. However, there was no regard for properly managing the program of participants once they incurred the second injury. Therefore, the cost ballooned for failing to properly have any rehabilitation options and police those receiving a weekly welfare check.

Once the Americans for Disabilities Act passed in 1990, of course, there was no public policy purpose to keeping the program going, and it was discontinued. But in each state, the runoff liability to participants continues to be paid by annual assessments on all employers.

CHAPTER 10

Public Finance Tidbits

Over the years, I enjoyed gathering little tidbits about decision making in public finance, the small pieces of information that are interesting and colorful. Here are a few of them.

Over the many years of practicing public finance, I came to appreciate that most professionals, whether elected officials or investment bankers or accountants or other consultants, are straightforward, honest, and competent. Every so often, however, I met individuals who are not only smart but naturally have a talent for the legislative practice and public finance. They adjust to the financial requirements rather than be guided by political polling. This chapter introduces you to several smart-thinking natural professionals.

Gilman Family in Connecticut

In the 1950s, the state of Connecticut had determined it needed to participate in the Interstate Highway Program due to federal funds under the Eisenhower initiative being available. It had done all the preliminary planning and engineering work for the highway connection from the New York border to New Haven, but the state legislature had not passed the bond financing legislation. Why? The answer would reside with the chair of the House Transportation Committee, a Mr. Gilman from the town of Gilman in southeastern Connecticut (north of New London, Connecticut).

The Gilman family (for which the town was named) came to Connecticut as Jewish immigrants in the late 1800s. They had started as peddlers in the rag and junk business. When football became a popular sport, the Gilmans reconfigured their business to stuff the rags into canvas. From that, they became the leading maker of football practice dummies.

A map of Connecticut was brought to the highway planning meeting. At that meeting, Mr. Gilman asked to see that map and then commented that the plans of the Expressway weren't going far enough east. He proceeded to draw a line extending it easterly and northerly rather than directly east past New London. His line went near Gilman, providing easy ingress and egress for trucks transporting football dummies and proceeded farther east and southerly to Rhode Island. There, it would connect with the interstate in that state. Thus, the interstate highway, rather than stopping at New Haven, extended all the way through southeastern Connecticut to Providence, a linkage inherently necessary to open up the Cape to New York and even Washington citizens. With the map configured as he suggested, the enabling bond act passed. The fact that Mr. Gilman's business benefitted and that southeastern Connecticut become available for increased business relocation was smart legislating.

Please read Appendix C, which describes other creative tidbits related to tolling.

Ned Regan in New York State

Public finance practice is, of course, financing for state and local governments, and it is both a political and financial business managed by elected officials or by their appointees. Because of that, it provides interesting intrigues of persuasion as well as "natural" talents in finance.

Ned Regan was elected in 1972 as a Republican County Executive of Eric County in New York State during a period in which the county's general fund budget was barely balanced. At the same time, its expenses were increasing, particularly as it assumed functions formerly provided by the city of Buffalo (such as the public hospital). Being in the family beer distribution business, Ned was naturally cost conscious and not inclined to increase taxes or borrowing. Ned was elected as a Republican and promised significant cost cutting.

Bernie Bober, of Ehrlich Bober, was the managing partner of the investment banking firm that dominated the short-term tax-exempt note market and was retained to "roll over" the county notes coming due. After hiring me as his counsel, Bernie and I went over the budget and concluded there was little leeway for reducing expenditures. The rating agencies anticipated effecting a major reduction in the county's rating. This would impose a high rate of interest on the notes unless the government took action.

In our first meeting with Ned, whom neither of us had met before, we told him he should consider a tax increase. After an hour or so, he thanked us. The next day he publicly surprised us by recommending that tax increase then and successfully effected its passage.

Ned went on to be elected the state's comptroller in 1979. In that position, he inherited what was called the Spring Borrowing. That meant every spring, the state of New York had to be in the short-term note market to cover its state aid obligation to municipalities. That amount had escalated from about $3 billion to almost $5 billion. In effect and in fact, this was an accumulated state general fund deficit.[58]

As the state's comptroller, Ned was provided a straightforward memo of law in 1989 from me attached to a financial analysis prepared by Ted Beason of J.P. Morgan. It recommended the creation of a new state borrowing authority to be known as the Local Government Assistance Corporation and the permanent bonding of that seasonal short-term notes by long-term bonds. This would eliminate the annual Spring Borrowing practice.[59]

Ned recommended the program to the Democratic governor and, with his endorsement, the legislature passed the bonding legislation, thus creating that special finance entity to permanently fund this deficit. The governor stated that "state leaders, credit rating agencies, and civic financial monitoring groups have all hailed this initiative as a long overdue fiscal reform."

Ned's natural fiscal instincts were displayed throughout his career, but his political instincts sometimes failed him.[60] He was the natural Republican to run for state governor on the Republican ticket in 1982, but that year, Ed Koch ran for governor as a Democrat. Mayor Ed Koch had been an extremely popular mayor of New York City. Ned didn't think he could compete in attracting money to campaign in New York where Democrats were dominant, so he chose to remain on the ticket as comptroller. He had not anticipated that an upstart from Queens, Mario Cuomo, would defeat Koch in the Democratic primary. An unknown Republican candidate, Lewis Lehrman, my Yale classmate and founder of Rite Aid drug stores, almost beat Cuomo. Many people in New York believed Ned would have beat Cuomo if he had run.[61]

Joe Lhota of New York City

Another talented public finance professional is Joe Lhota, who recently resigned his second tenure as Governor Cuomo's appointed chairman of the New York Metropolitan Transit Authority (MTA). He resigned his first appointment by Democrat Governor Andrew Cuomo to run as the Republican candidate for mayor of New York City.[62]

Prior to this appointment, Joe had been an investment banker and then served in various roles in Mayor Giuliani's administration, rising to first deputy mayor. For many years, he had been my colleague as a financial advisor and then an underwriter representing a major

Connecticut Authority. Over the years, the Authority had issued several billion dollars of bonds for financing low- and moderate-priced housing. Whether as chairman of the MTA or as a young financial advisor, Joe brought to the table a straightforward financial acumen that was expressed in simple terms. He was born in the Bronx, the son of a New York City policeman and grandson of a New York firefighter and taxicab driver with Czech and Jewish lineage.

In each of his career positions, Joe proved to be creative, hardworking, and effective. As deputy mayor in 1997, he retained me to assist in drafting a new financing structure for the varied capital structures to be built by New York City. It would become known as the New York Transitional Finance Authority (TFA) and would pledge the city sales and income tax in a way that would modernize the terminology and apply the concept of "securitization."

The right to receive the sales and income tax would be sold to a separate purpose authority to issue bonds to finance the city capital needs. This structure needed serious legal analysis in each state to assure it did not run afoul of constitutional restrictions and to comply with the ring-fencing requirement of the rating agencies.

"Securitization" was a term used in corporate finance, so Joe seized on that as the perfect nomenclature. Why? Because it meant that when the city requested ratings from the rating agencies for this structure, the city could access those rating agency professionals who were charged with analyzing cash flow rather than general credit. In other words, the rating agency's analysis would focus on the amount of the sales tax and income tax received in previous years. From there, it would apply its algorithm to derive a rating that reflected the debt service coverage available for the bonds issued. The basic assumption? Past results were indicative of future results. There would be *no* focus on whether or not the city was balancing its general fund budget each year or incurring regular general fund deficits. To be sure, there would be a focus on the structure to ensure it was legally fenced off from any city insolvency.

New York City had come a long way since 1975. With budget oversight and mayors including Mayor Giuliani touting strong fiscal records, the timing for this structure was ideal. (Upon the establishment of the authority, a taxpayer challenged the structure, but based on our briefing, the Court of Appeals upheld the statute so that market risk was eliminated.) The first meeting with the rating agencies ended quickly when Joe realized the professionals from the rating agencies were the traditional general obligation experts. We politely asked the "securitization group" to manage the next meeting. That group had been first formed when the credit card companies wanted to market bonds secured by future receipts of credit card holders. It would require the rating agencies to analyze the creditworthiness of that segment of cash flow.

Years later, the rating agencies were severely criticized when, for the bond issues with collateralized mortgage obligations, they used the same algorithms to rate payments on mortgages as they had used for credit card payments. What did the rating agencies miss? The answer is the basic fact that there was a fundamental underwriting difference between those college attendees and business officials who freely received and used credit cards and those who were receiving mortgages.[63]

In any case, TFA received a triple-A credit rating that it enjoys today, and full credit goes to Joe Lhota. He took advantage of the modernization and inherent value of this approach. Based on that success, I tried to convince other clients who had a high rating to consider segregating one of the revenue sources (sales or income tax) to achieve or maintain a triple A. Surprisingly, certain clients (including the state of Connecticut) refused to go forward for reasons I still can't appreciate. Only after Connecticut's triple-A rating was reduced two grades did the state's treasurer consider the "securitization" approach.

CHAPTER 11

What Is the Tenth Amendment?

In other chapters that discussed tax-exempt bonds, I mentioned the federal treasury's view—that is, the market differential between the interest at the corporate rate and the tax-exempt rates is a federal subsidy. In fact, the title of a federal act exempting the interest on bonds issued to finance mortgages for first-time homeowners and low- and moderate-income earners and families was called the Mortgage Subsidy Housing Tax Act.

This chapter discusses cases that focus on interpretations of the Tenth Amendment concerning federal vs. states' rights.

Thinking through that "subsidy" concept, I conclude this: Treasury officials believe exemption of taxation on governmental (state, public authorities, and municipalities) bonds is granted by the federal government; it's not a basic right of each state's sovereignty.[65] The opposite view is the law of the land and known as the Tenth Amendment,[66] as originally contemplated by Alexander Hamilton.

The provision is stated this way:

The authority of States to borrow money, like the authority to raise revenues through taxation, is a core aspect of State

> sovereignty. State and local governments must have access to capital markets in order to carry out their essential function of protecting and promoting the health, safety, and welfare of their citizens. By issuing municipal bonds, States and their political subdivisions are able to raise funds for costly projects that benefit State citizens over extended periods of time without having to depend entirely on tax revenues. In the absence of municipal bonds, many important State and local government initiatives would have to be delayed or cancelled.
>
> Alexander Hamilton, perhaps the foremost authority on American public finance, observed that credit "is of the greatest consequence to every country." Alexander Hamilton, *Public Credit* in 2 The Works of Alexander Hamilton 294 (Henry Cabot Lodge ed. 1971) (1904). In *The Federalist,* Hamilton wrote that "individual States should possess an independent and uncontrollable authority to raise their own revenues for the supply of their own wants," and thus "an attempt by the national government to abridge (the States) in the exercise of [that authority] would be a violent assumption of power, unwarranted by any article or clause of its Constitution." *The Federalist* No. 32 (A. Hamilton).[67]

Supreme Court Cases Fuel Discussion

This contradictory view of a basic principle underlying federal-state relationships can be best explained in reading these two opinions rendered by the Supreme Court of the United States (SCOTUS): *South Carolina v. Baker*, 485 US 505 (1988) and *United Haulers Ass'n., Inc. v. Oneida-Herkimer Solid Waste Management Authority*, 550 US 330 (2007). In these cases, we're focusing on SCOTUS's affirmation of the basic sovereign power of the states to issue bonds as an indispensable alternative to taxation. This provides a means of attaining cash to carry out the states' essential function of protecting and promoting the health, safety, and welfare of their citizens.

The South Carolina case involved the fact that a federal statute mandated a tax on the interest on municipal bonds unless those bonds were registered to the owner. Previously, most bonds were issued and traded in bearer form, thereby precluding automatically accessing information on the owner. The purpose of passing such a law was to preclude using coupon bonds to launder illegal money gained from drug and prostitution and to engage in those and other illegal transactions. (Today, the same issue of deception is raised in connection with bitcoin and other cryptocurrency transactions.)

Clearly, the federal government has a valid interest in regulating and preventing this kind of activity. Unfortunately, the states challenged this assertion of federal power over its sovereign power to issue bonds free of federal taxation and lost the argument. SCOTUS ruled that this statute to curtail illegal transactions was not a direct assault on state sovereignty and well within the federal power.

However, in a footnote, the concept of reciprocal tax immunity was discarded as well. That led many commentators to conclude that the constitutional Tenth Amendment argument precluding federal taxation on the interest of the state and municipal bonds was lost. Since the statute did not involve such an issue, the footnote is properly described as "dicta," which means it had not been the subject of a case or controversy judicial review on the merits. Stated another way, reciprocal immunity has been regarded as a basic constitutional principle. That means the federal government could not tax the bonds of the sovereign states, and the states could not tax the bonds of the sovereign federal government.

The South Carolina case properly recognized that this principle was not absolute. In other words, there are financings that are readily apparent as an abuse of state power rather than an essential element of sovereignty. Thereafter, the Mortgage Subsidy Act, the Private Activity Act, and the Tax-Exempt Responsibility Act (TEFRA) were passed.

These acts limited the types of bonds that could be issued by states for housing, for industrial development, and for arbitrage as discussed in Chapter 12.

Validity of Tenth Amendment Defense

Fortunately, for those who believe in Alexander Hamilton's view, two subsequent cases strongly suggest the Tenth Amendment defense is still valid. (I believe that footnote in South Carolina will be treated as outdated dicta if there is a direct attempt to repeal the interest exemption on municipal bonds.) The *United Haulers* case reflects SCOTUS upholding the basic rule of state sovereignty when the state itself or its political subdivisions are participating directly in an acknowledged public purpose—in this case, the collection and disposal of solid waste. Therefore, the state could validly allow a municipality to require all solid waste in its jurisdiction to be collected and transported to its own waste disposal facility. From there, it would be processed to produce energy for sale to an investor-owned utility.

SCOTUS upheld that the flow control of the "commerce" of solid waste disposal did not violate the commerce clause that prohibits states from discriminating against interstate trade. The haulers claimed an unfettered right to take the solid waste they collected anywhere in or out of state to a proper landfill or waste-to-energy plant, and they challenged this "flow control ordinance." In a similar example of a commerce clause violation, states have passed laws banning, regulating, or taxing milk products from other states as a protective measure for its in-state milk production industry. A recent solid waste disposal case had held that a municipality mandating the solid waste "flow" to a privately owned landfill was unconstitutional under the commerce clause. However in the more recent case *United Haulers* case, SCOTUS upheld the sovereignty of states to fulfill the health needs of citizens by the sovereign owning and operating of its own waste-to-energy facility and its restriction on flow disposal of solid waste to that governmental facility.[68]

In *Dept. of Revenue of Ky. v. Davis*, 553 US 328, (2008), a couple living in Kentucky challenged the Kentucky law. This law required the couple to pay a state income tax on bonds they owned from Ohio and other states. However, the state law exempted interest in Kentucky bonds, the couple claimed that the commerce clause prohibits states from discriminating against interstate commerce. In effect, any state does this by protecting and enhancing the value of its bonds over bonds of other states.

The *Davis* case was first decided by the Kentucky Supreme Court, holding the law was unconstitutional. As a partner in the firm with a corporate affiliation with the National Association of State Treasurers (NAST), I persuaded its board to file an amicus (advisory and voluntary) brief on behalf of NAST. It requested SCOTUS take the case on appeal based on the points made in our brief. SCOTUS accepted the case even though it would normally have waited for challenges and decisions in other states before taking one on, based on an alleged violation of the commerce clause.

On behalf of NAST, we also prepared an amicus brief and counseled on the oral arguments. My partner, Ken Roberts, and I received an award from NAST for that service.

SCOTUS was clear in its opinion that the Kentucky law was an exercise of state sovereignty in carrying out its governmental purpose of raising revenues for financing facilities such as hospitals, water and service plants, and schools owned by governments and available to the general public. Therefore, any state is allowed to permit its bonds (and those of its political subdivisions) to be exempt from its state income tax of the interest while taxing the interest on such bonds of other states.[70]

Right to Issue Tax-Exempt Bonds

What is critical to both the *Haulers* and the *Davis* cases is that *SCOTUS reaffirmed the power of the states as sovereigns to issue tax-exempt bonds.*[71]

In 2018, the federal government passed an act eliminating the tax exemption on "advance refunding." But is this restriction constitutional? Is it an essential part of the states' sovereignty to be permitted to issue bonds for this purpose based on *United Haulers* and *Davis*? Or is it a corrective action of the federal government to prevent an "arbitrage abuse" as defined in Chapter 12? The issue is ripe for litigation, but so far, states are focused on repealing that and other provisions of the Tax Cuts and Jobs Act signed by President Donald Trump on December 22, 2017.

The federal treasury continues to express the view that tax exemption is a federal subsidy; and it's just a matter of federal tax policy whether state bonds are exempt from federal interest. But these two recent cases suggest the Supreme Court, as currently composed, would rule that such federal taxation was unconstitutional because it would be infringing on state sovereignty in cases where the bonds are to provide funds for a traditional public purpose well.

The next chapter confronts the complex nature of that principle —that is, state officials can be creative, and certain type issues can be treated as an "abuse" of the exercise of sovereign power.

CHAPTER 12

What Is Arbitrage?

This chapter provides insight into the technical issues involved in tax-exempt bonds and the recurring battles between the U.S. Treasury and state governments to balance their competing interests.[72]

Basically, states claim that a federal tax on interest on municipal bonds is unconstitutional under the Tenth Amendment as a violation of state sovereignty. If imposed, the tax triggers the reciprocal power of the state to enforce its own tax on the interest on the U.S. Treasury obligation. The U.S. Treasury claims that the interest exemption on state bonds from federal income taxation is a federal subsidy. Since income tax was first imposed in 1916, some federal statutes to tax interest on governmental bonds for certain projects and programs have been considered "abuses" of state power. But to date, no statute eliminating the interest exemption on traditional public purpose state and municipal bonds has been passed. The following are examples of the evolution of federal legislation passed by Congress to curb these perceived "abuses." Despite having crafted several of those issues before the legislation, I concur that the proper balance between state and federal interest has been met.

Ohio Example

In 1960, *The Bond Buyer* headlined an irresponsible proposal by Ohio's treasurer in which the state would issue $100 million in tax-exempt bonds to finance a $10 million capital improvement program. It would invest the balance in an investment fund of taxable securities with a rate well over the tax-exempt bond interest rate, thus providing a profit sufficient to amortize all of the debt service on that bond issuance without raising taxes.[73] Interest-free capital to Ohio's treasury—what is now understood in the municipal market to be a classic arbitrage—involves borrowing in one market to invest in another market for profit.

While I regarded the Ohio Treasurer's proposal as an abuse, I was chagrined to realize years before I had counseled on a similar financing. I had structured an "investment sinking fund"[74] providing Connecticut's state treasurer with the annual option of redeeming the bonds or investing the amount of the $4 million debt service appropriation in taxable securities. Without concern, I did that as an economically efficient plan that was well vetted with potential bidders and bought at a public sale. That issue consisted of $80 million of term bonds with a twentieth-year maturity and $4,000,000 a year sinking fund debt amortization. At that time, the concept of arbitrage wasn't a part of the public finance lexicon.

What I proposed in Connecticut was, in spirit, a financing structure no different from what the Ohio treasurer was proposing. The original proceeds of $100 million offerings had been used to build low- and moderate-income housing projects in several cities, which was a proper public purpose without question. However, the "abuse of arbitrage" occurs by holding back the payoff of tax-exempt bonds by investing in higher treasuries.[75]

Suffice it to say that the U.S. Treasury immediately, and rightly so, recognized the Ohio proposal as the state's "abuse of arbitrage" by proposing a flagrant opportunity to "game" federal/state coordinated financial governance. How did the U.S. Treasury clamp down on this as a taxable "arbitrage" transaction? It secured passage of a federal statute and drafted strict regulations afterward. What has emerged is a complex set of rules and regulations and a standard of code embedded as a covenant in all tax-exempt transactions to prevent "arbitrage." If the practice happens inadvertently, the statute builds in provisions requiring rebates of any interest profit by the issuer to the treasury.[76]

However, my public finance practice continued to include "arbitrage" transactions until the logical legal extension of "arbitrage" was clarified and further treasury regulations developed. The following two examples of tax-exempt transactions in Brookhaven and Bridgeport were opportunities deemed proper as public purposes but applied (without prejudice) to deals closed before treasury regulations broadened the definition of investments once the "arbitrage" details were fully analyzed.

Brookhaven Example

On a Thursday morning in 1970, I received a call from the town attorney of Brookhaven, New York, a Long Island client of the firm. The attorney requested immediate assistance on an unusual opportunity the town government wanted to pursue. Charged with building office buildings for federal agencies, the federal General Service Administration (GSA) wanted bids to build and lease an office building that would house hundreds of employees of the Internal Revenue Service.[77] Could Brookhaven bid for that project? Could the town propose to issue general obligation bonds because it would bring new jobs to the area as a public purpose? Or was the transaction unconstitutional due to lending credit for a private purpose being explicitly banned by the New York State constitution?

At the time, I was chairman of the New York Municipal Law Section of the New York State Bar Association. I was becoming an expert on the New York local finance law, representing the Hawkins practice of bond counsel for many New York counties, towns, villages, cities, and fire, flood, and school districts. That afternoon, I called back Brookhaven's attorney to say it would take a special act of the New York State legislature to authorize a project such as this.

There was no explicit authority under the town law establishing that kind of purpose. However, a controlling practical and legal precedent existed that would permit such a transaction. A special law authorized the county of Albany to build and finance a building (Albany Mall) for lease to house state employees.[78] That law had been challenged as invalid under several sections of the New York constitution, but it had been validated by the Court of Appeals, the state's highest court.[79] Based on that, it didn't seem to be a big stretch that a town could be authorized by law to build and finance a building for lease to the federal government.

The next day, Friday, Brookhaven retained my firm, which meant I could draft the special legislation. The GSA-scheduled bidding process required the bidders to be qualified by the following Thursday. That meant a special act had to be passed on Monday or Tuesday!

All the political powers of the town, the county, and the governor's office worked with me to finalize this draft over the weekend. Sunday night, the town board met and passed a home rule message requesting that the legislation (as we had drafted it) be approved by the state legislature. The draft was approved in Brookhaven Sunday night and sent to Albany on Monday. The state legislature passed it Monday, and it was signed by the governor on Tuesday.

That's how the town was able to submit its bid on time. And it won the bid because its tax-exempt borrowing costs were less than any private developer could offer. It also successfully bonded and built the building to lease to the GSA. Again, its taxexempt borrowing cost was the lowest compared with developers who had to calculate rent based on taxable financing. This quick action served to provide employment for hundreds of people in the Brookhaven region.

Subsequently, though, the U.S. Treasury implemented a regulation ruling that such a transaction was "arbitrage." It regulated that any unconditional lease obligation of the federal government to pay debt service constituted an investment in an obligation. It was like investing in a treasury note. Ironically, the building would house employees of the Internal Revenue Service, but despite this public purpose, calling the transaction an "abuse of arbitrage" was a logical conclusion.

Bridgeport Example

A second example also resulted in the treasury closing a "loophole" in its arbitrage regulations after the deal closed. The city of Bridgeport, Connecticut, had decided to interview bond counsel firms regarding a proposal to issue its general obligation bonds to finance unfunded current accrued liability of its employee pension trust fund. Pension bonds are those issued by a state or municipality to discharge an accrued legal liability to a pension fund for its employees by depositing the proceeds of those bonds in the pension fund. The pension fund then invests in accordance with its payout schedule to the beneficiaries.

I had to present a proposal for my firm to serve as its bond counsel. I was interviewed before the city council in its ornate council chambers with its seating for more than three hundred people. In any of my Connecticut presentations to state or municipal issuers, I often encountered a natural animosity against this New York lawyer. So from the start of this interview, I said I was born in Hartford, raised in Norwich and West Hartford, and was a lifelong resident of the Long Island Sound beach in New London, Connecticut. I remarked that my grandfather first lived in Bridgeport before becoming a successful businessman in Norwich. I presented myself as a hometown boy after all, with my New York law firm barely mentioned.

In the interview, a council person noted that, from my written proposal, it didn't seem that I had experience with pension bonds, so why should I be selected? Good question. I responded that Bridgeport would be among the first issuers in the nation of this type of bond; neither New York nor Connecticut law firms had experience with it either. Then I emphasized that we were here today because, for several years, the city council and mayor had failed to budget well. They had not appropriated the amount that the actuarial experts had been reporting as the proper contribution amount. As a result, the city had "an accumulated general fund deficit," which is the amount needing to be bonded to bring that fund and its corresponding pension fund to current balance.

With that fact in mind, I recounted that I had several comparable retainers: (1) to fund general fund accumulated deficits of New York City during its fiscal crisis, (2) "deficit funding" bonds to balance the city of Yonkers general fund and prevent that city from filing for bankruptcy, and (3) state of Connecticut "economic recovery notes" (a perfumed-up word for deficit funding) to carry the general fund during an economic downturn when anticipated taxes were less than general fund expenditures.[80] That triple analogy hit home, and the city of Bridgeport hired me that day.

Shortly after, the U.S. Treasury reviewed the structure that allowed a state or municipality to issue tax-exempt bonds to finance an accumulated pension fund deficit, thereby permitting the pension fund trustee to invest those proceeds in taxable obligations at higher rates. A legal distinction could be made, arguing that the pension fund was a trust fund separate from the state/city. Therefore, the obligation of the city was contractual with an entity independent of the city. Hawkins was not challenged on its opinion on those bonds being tax exempt. However, the treasury quickly adopted regulations banning future so-called tax-exempt pension obligations.

The technical distinction created difficult webs for tax attorneys because the pension fund of employees is separate from the state or city. Hence, the treasury rules today require tracing the use of grants by the state for *any* purpose. That includes traditional grants for a city's infrastructure construction to ensure that money was not invested but was spent for that purpose within a reasonable time.

Budget Balancing by Surrey

In 1961, Stanley Surrey, a professor of Harvard Law School, was appointed Assistant Deputy Secretary of the Treasury for Tax Policy.[81] By force of his erudite writings, Surrey transformed the federal budget process into a sleight of hand game of "scoring," which meant the playing field was purposely restricted or sized to the federal budget only. Hence, rather than including the direct effect of the federal budget on the wallet of the individual taxpayers, his approach worked to balance the federal budget without adjusting for the direct effect on state budgets.

The most direct example of such obfuscation or sophistry is that Surrey scored the interest exemption as an expenditure of the federal budget.[82] A law to eliminate it would increase the interest rate revenues to the federal government but become a resulting cost increase to states. Accordingly, it would be a budget buster to taxpayers at the local level.

What is the legal theory supporting this? Taxing interest on a sovereign state's bonds is exercising a power to destroy that sovereignty, and it could be countered by the state's taxing federal treasury obligation. After Surrey, interest on bonds (except for arbitrage, certain housing finance purposes, and certain industrial aid bonds) remain exempt from federal income taxes but are scored as a tax expenditure of the federal budget. It would be as if the federal government appropriated the money and disregarded the fact that wealthy tax-avoidance citizens would shift to another tax shelter.

At one point, officials in President Obama's administration had suggested that the top 28 percent income brackets should be ineligible to exempt the interest on its holdings of municipal bonds. The cost of borrowing by state and local governments would therefore be higher, thus making the proposal a huge tax increase. Why? Because state and local governments would be required to pass that higher differential of interest onto taxpayers. Ironically, though, high-income taxpayers would simply shift to other tax shelters, and the treasury would not receive any "scoring" benefit.[83]

Proper Power Play

When Ohio's state treasurer announced such a bond plan, the U.S. Treasury successfully rushed amendments to the tax code provisions banning arbitrage and, like any federal program, its interpretation took on a life of its own. In turn, this spawned a whole new practice of tax compliance advisors. No one had considered such an explicit arbitrage plan as promoting a public purpose; people agreed it was an improper practice. There was no substantive policy objection when pension and lease-secured bonds, as described above, were brought within the ban. State and municipalities could not object since the practice was understood to be a logical extension of the policy to curb the "abuse" of arbitrage.

Interestingly, from the standpoint of developing a national policy to avoid potential bankruptcy of some major cities and states, interest in permitting a tax-exempt borrowing program to fund the unfunded accrued liability of pension funds in return for some compromise in the benefits vested has been renewed.

World of Workman's Compensation

Within the finance world of workman's compensation, a straightforward "arbitrage" activity still exists. Thus, when there is a two- or three-year period of increased unemployment, the state/federal insurance program of paying out for a few months' compensation until a new job kicks in, and the funds reserved for such contingency after a period are exhausted. By law, the federal treasury extends an interest-free loan to the state for nine months. If it's not paid back, it then becomes an interest-bearing loan at the federal rate and retroactive to the beginning of the initial drawdown.

In 1994, the state of Connecticut had a billion-dollar loan outstanding. As the state's bond counsel, I conceived of and structured a solution. Rather than subjecting the state to paying the federal government the retroactive federal interest rate, the state issued a billion-dollar bond. This paid off the federal loan and saved the state millions on the differential.

Other states, of course, immediately recognized this transaction as an economically smart option. But because October 1st was the deadline to pay off the federal loan, some legislatures couldn't get the "gist" of the deal to pass the necessary bond authorization in time. This included the Commonwealth of Massachusetts, which would have saved the equivalent of the entire administrative cost of government employees in that year.

That happened in the 1990s when the federal interest rate was considerably higher than today. Of course, interest on a billion dollars for nine months adds up to real money. At this time, though, the federal lending rate is so low, the program has become problematic. Putting the billion-dollar Connecticut bond issue into the market with an October 1st "all or none" deadline exemplified how well the tax-exempt market could function given its assortment of variable rate, fixed rate (some enhanced by insurance), or letters of credit needed to attract investors.

The federal treasury has had to expand, redraft, revise, and maintain constant vigilance. As a result, the arbitrage rules have become extremely complex; a whole subcategory of tax specialists must be retained for arbitrage compliance and rebate calculations.

My reason for strongly supporting the tax-exempt bonds is this: That feature supports a multibillion-dollar finance market. It attracts wealthy individuals and affiliates who buy based on their assessment of investment of risk and ratings. To substitute this with a federal subsidy program would sacrifice the market feature and create a political quagmire—that is, who would determine which interest subsidy should apply to what issuers?

Reasons exist to preclude the States, their municipalities, and public authorities from issuing tax-exempt bonds that "game" the system, such as bonds to build $100 million manufacturing plants, bonds to finance housing for wealthy individuals, bonds to "arbitrage" the differential in taxable and tax-exempt rates. However, the present tax-exempt bonding for public purposes such as water or sewer systems, transportation facilities, or public power should remain if we are to preserve the sovereignty of states and their ability to finance those capital structures.

CHAPTER 13

What Is Bond Disclosure?

This chapter addresses regulatory differences between municipal bond and corporate stock offerings as well as the development of an application format that's still in use today.

In today's legal climate, corporate offerings need to be prefiled and reviewed by the Securities and Exchange Commission (SEC). This organization regulates the form and substance of what is in the documents as mandated statutory disclosure, while only the so-called section 10b-5 antifraud statute applies to state and municipal bond offerings. In fact, the Tower Amendment[84] statutorily precludes the SEC from requiring registration or prefiling of any municipal offering document.

Only recently has the SEC found the ways and means to achieve SEC oversight and enforcement over state and municipal issuers through its regulation of investment bankers and financial advisors. It has also found indirect ways to control through initial offering statements and ongoing disclosure agreements between issuer and initial buyers of bonds.[85]

Market Shutdown Caused Requirement for Better Documentation

In 1975, because of New York City's fiscal crisis, the market for state and municipal bonds became obsessed with the need for information about every state and local issuer. As a practical matter, the national market shut down for New York issuers and most of the northeast without first receiving "full disclosure."

Municipal "revenue" bonds were traditionally marketed through an abbreviated document that related the annual revenues expected to be received. These revenues were to operate the facilities owned by, say, the New York Power Authority. The document included details about the service area and the capital improvements program underway as well as the customer base—but little else. The market relied primarily on the rating and rating agencies for due diligence of details for both revenue and general obligation tax-exempt bond offerings. Mostly, the general obligation bonds of a state and its municipalities were sold by public sale. This included a "statement of essential facts" pertaining to outstanding bonds, percentage of debt limit exhausted, valuation of assessable property, and other summary statistical information.

Before 1975, there had been no disclosure regarding the general fund operating budget and certainly nothing about management. In fact, nothing more had been required. After 1975, though, any revenue or general obligation offering required more. That's when the role of bond counsel and the investment bankers expanded significantly. Preparing a disclosure document became a lengthy process. As a result, negotiated sales rather than public competitive sales became the norm for large issues.

This affected me because I was hired by my two most important clients, the state of Connecticut and the county of Westchester, to review offering statements. I had to render 10b-5 opinions (a standard closing document in a corporate transaction) to affirm that the documents contained no material omission and all material matters had been included.

State of Connecticut

I was also retained by the state of Connecticut to supervise the preparations of a preliminary offering statement that would satisfy the credit markets in this new post-1975 era. To allow such supervision, the state of Connecticut accepted full responsibility for making available the officers and knowledgeable personnel. The Hawkins team included me and then associate Eric Peterson, who took notes.

First, I reviewed the disclosure statements of major revenue bond issues such as the Power Authority, the Delaware Bridge Authority, and the Connecticut Expressway. Then I looked at registration filings of corporate bond offerings and concluded I could create my own improved format as follows:

1) State who the issuer is—details about governance, and the statistical detail such as population, major employers, and products or services in the state such as nuclear submarines at Electric Boat, Sikorsky helicopters, and Pratt & Whitney aircraft and its several headquartered insurance companies.
2) Summarize the amount of the overall debt and then state the nature of the debt being offered and the authorized but unissued backlog.
3) Add other liability matters such as pension obligations.
4) Summarize expenditures and sources of revenues, including taxes and other matters related to the general fund and the budgeting process.
5) Describe the professionals involved, such as the auditors, underwriters, and financial advisors as well as the law firm rendering the opinion that the bonds are valid.

This approach proved to be logical and straightforward, just as a bank officer would require if you walked into the bank requesting a loan. You'd tell the banker who you are, what you do, how much debt you have, and your resources to repay that debt. You'd say how much debt you need now and in the near future as well as the budget process and results over recent years. Last, you would include an appendix, the financial statements as audited. This practical, procedural way of disclosure was accepted by the separately elected state's treasurer, who was also the state chief fiscal officer for the state.

After many weeks of working on the documentation, we successfully sold the Connecticut bonds.

County of Westchester

Next, I worked with the county of Westchester with then-associate Marty Geiger assisting me. I had the benefit of working with Vincent Matrone, the county's chief fiscal officer, who later became a successful investment banker in Texas (where the climate permitted him to play golf year round). Matrone fully supported my approach and made sure the right personnel were available to us. We followed the Connecticut format to prepare the documentation.

The Westchester County bond issue, with a comprehensive new official statement, became the first issue in New York to be offered, marketed, and bought by investors nationwide since New York's fiscal crisis. The governor, state comptroller, and county executive had previously agreed to have Westchester be first to go to market, because it had the best credit to reopen the national market.

Sample Document Standard Set

As the law firm evolved as both bond counsel for the county and the New York City Municipal Assistant Corporation, Hawkins had expertise on the disclosure requirements required by the market at the time. And those officials knew it, too! I received thank-you calls from many of them for reopening the New York municipal bond market.

Of course, it was clear that developing a decent disclosure document was mostly symbolic since rating agencies, investors, and every portfolio buyer was aware that Westchester was among the top two or three richest counties in the nation. More important, only since post–World War II had the county started borrowing rather than "paying as you go" for most capital improvements.

My partner, Don Robinson, followed the Connecticut and Westchester format to produce a sample standard for the Practicing Law Institute. That way, the rest of the bond community fell into line to provide a standardized format still used to this day. Because of its acceptance in the national marketplace, as a practical matter, this model preempted the SEC from creating an internal task force to propose its own format or push for the repeal of the Tower Amendment to require prefiling or some form of registration.

Ironically, the SEC still alleges that municipal offerings are not up to corporate standards. Yet to my knowledge, there has never been an SEC taskforce that has formally reviewed what would or could be proper municipal disclosure. In effect, they have totally accepted the format of the original post-1975 offering proposal for Connecticut. Certainly, the SEC has been kept busy with the Enron fraud, the collapse of the securitized mortgage market, and other corporate failings, as well as the Dodd-Frank legislation. For the most part, these have effectively taken the focus off the municipal market.

On that first financing in Connecticut, I had a memorable experience with then Governor Ella Grasso. Before finalizing an official statement in this new detailed format, the underwriters were concerned that the Securities Exchange Commission would be reading this new formatted document. (The SEC had prepared a report heavily criticizing the underwriters of New York City Bonds and Notes for failing to ask the officers of the city where the revenues were coming from to pay off the billions of revenue anticipation notes.) The big disclosure issue during that period in Connecticut (which was in serious stress balancing its general fund budget) was whether the newly elected Governor Grasso was ready to announce her support for an income tax. As the group of bankers sat around a table discussing how to find that out, one banker "friend" of mine said the state's bond counsel should do that diligence. He was looking at me with a serious smirk. Fortunately, I responded that, yes, I would. I then explained to the group that I knew her quite well and had spent hours in her office when she was secretary of state. Why? The monthly minutes of the state bond commission had to be filed with the secretary of state to be official and for any spending authorized by the SBC to be legal. As a practical matter, right after every meeting I took those minutes into her office for filing and to get her signature on a certificate of filing. She would always want details on each bond authorization and then usually would inquire about my family or other personal issues, and we'd chat. She knew I was from Hartford and also knew my uncle, a state legislator, and his son David Borden, who would go on to lead the state's highest court.

Anyway, shortly after meeting with the bankers, I called the governor's office and requested a meeting. When her assistant said I was on the phone requesting a meeting, she told me to come right over. After the usual greetings, I explained I had an important question to ask. The answer to it could help us decide what to say in the preliminary offering document.

Here's the question I asked Governor Grasso: "Are you contemplating the introduction of a state income tax?" Without hesitation, she responded, "No f—ing way" (articulating the left-out letters) and said, "You can print that." On hearing the answer, the bankers decided to not include anything about the income tax, and I concurred. Why? Had we written that the governor was not contemplating the introduction of an income tax, I thought it would be necessary to add to the end of that sentence words to the effect that "no assurance can be given that the governor will not change her views in the course of the upcoming budget proceedings." We decided to stay away from the subject altogether. In reading that caveat, I'm sure the governor would have accused me of either not listening or even lying, as her answer had been unequivocal.

CHAPTER 14

What Is Venture Capital?

Since the start of my financial law practice in 1964, many new financial products and public purposes have been introduced to the municipal bond market. State and local government can only issue bonds to be used for a "public purpose," but that term has been expanded as the public perception of government has broadened. This chapter explains how that term is tied with the concept of venture capital.

Industrial Development Bonds[88] create new job opportunities; Pollution Control Bonds encourage private corporations to stop polluting waterways; Mortgage Subsidy Bonds assist in building housing for low- and moderate-income persons and first-time homeowners; Public-Private Partnership Bonds build facilities based on private and public skill sets.

One of the first unknown benefits of my practice at Hawkins was getting to work with Henry E. (Ike) Russell from New Britain, Connecticut, and a *Yale Law Review* editor. He was a public finance partner and had been counsel on the initial financing of the Connecticut Expressway as he knew Abe Ribicoff, then governor of Connecticut, also from New Britain, Connecticut. Ike Russell had established himself and his firm as the creative resourceful public finance confidant of George Conkling, who for more than forty years was the state's highly respected finance officer, relied on for budget and bonding purposes by both Democratic and Republican governors.

Perfect Match

As a Connecticut native and Yale graduate, I was the perfect match for taking on Connecticut matters. Being a "natural" around elected officials, I gained their confidences, especially as I would become well informed on the applicable law before rendering advice. In addition, I inherited a plethora of municipal bond issues (city, village, county, fire, flood and erosion districts) in New York from Gerry Fernandez. From Ike Russell, I was given state business in Alaska (as noted in Chapter 2 and 13 in Volume I) as well as in Connecticut. As a result, I became proficient in these three states—all with decidedly different approaches to public finance and state constitutional regimes.

When Connecticut had its constitutional convention in 1948, it removed any serious vestiges of municipal or state constitutional restrictions except forbidding private emoluments. In comparison, New York State held its 1938 constitutional convention and brought in numerous state and local constitutional restrictions, including a referendum for state debt, debt limits for municipalities, explicit requirements that municipalities must pledge their full "faith and credit" in incurring municipal debt, and on and on. Not anticipated by those well-educated delegates at the constitutional conventions were the twentieth-century demands to service a growing population that demanded creative, diverse, and expensive financial structuring.

This was true particularly in New York to circumvent the restrictions of the New York constitutional provisions. Circumventing these restrictions was supported and advocated by good government groups because the procedures to repeal constitutional provisions proved to be onerous. Thus, in New York, what did we get? John Mitchell's debt structure of "moral obligation," described in Appendix D of this book. If you recall, this shift happened after voters twice defeated general obligation bonds to finance low- and moderate-income residential rental housing projects despite the support of Governor Rockefeller and both parties.[89]

New Bond Concept

Bob Berdon, Connecticut's state treasurer, called me one day with a new bond concept he wanted me to draft. Bob Berdon and his brother were both New Haven lawyers practicing together when Tom Meskill was working on how best to balance his election ticket ethnically, as was the tradition in Connecticut. (The offices of governor, attorney general, secretary of state comptroller, and treasurer are all elected.) The Democratic Party had allocated the treasurer's spot to an African American while the Republican party, headed by Tom Meskill, determined someone of the Jewish faith was politically appropriate.
Not knowing there were two Berdons, Meskill wondered if Berdon would be interested. When a staff member called Bob Berdon, Bob delightedly accepted. It was only later after public announcements had been made that Meskill realized it was Bob's *brother* he knew and had wanted. Politically, though, it was too late to admit that kind of mistake.

It turned out that Bob Berdon, the "wrong" brother, became the best treasurer I'd ever had the pleasure to work with. He advanced the reach and respect of Connecticut public finance enormously; his brashness, boldness, intellect, and public awareness became a real force. He even arranged for the state itself to be allowed to trade on the Philadelphia Stock Exchange because he did *not* like paying the New York Stock Exchange trading fees.[90]

Treasurer Berdon asked me to draft legislation to authorize general obligation bonds of the state, with the proceeds to fund a "venture capital" fund. I didn't know what that was, since this happened well before Menlo Park, Apple, computers, and the internet developed. He said to me, "Look up the term 'venture capital'; the Bank of England is doing it."

In essence, Berdon asked me to draft legislation authorizing the state of Connecticut to issue its bonds that would be supported by the state's "faith and credit" pledge. Therefore, it would be paid by taxpayers' dollars coming from the state's sales or income tax. It would be deposited with Connecticut's Products Development Corporation, a new public authority, to make loans or invest with people or stocks in a private corporation proposing a new concept that might be commercially viable. The idea might be developed and a facility might then be built in Connecticut, thus providing new jobs. This new authority would become the "Shark Tank" for Connecticut entrepreneurs.

Private or Public Emolument?

In my mind, there was just to remote a link between the risky use of public money and the reality of a new business and employment in Connecticut. The *Roan* case in Connecticut had established it was not a private emolument for the state to issue bonds to make loans to private companies that are directly linked to using the bond proceeds to build manufacturing plants and thereby provide new employment. The court had held that this use of public funds to assist a company promising to provide more employment in the state "was not a private emolument" under that one restrictive constitutional clause. In other words, such a loan was a public purpose, and public use of public monies intended to create jobs for Connecticut residents. These Industrial Development Bonds were being issued in almost every state, but the hard-wire connection between a job and factory was clearer than what the state treasurer was proposing.

Delivering an unqualified opinion about the bond market to the state treasurer on the validity of such "venture capital" bonds was difficult. Treasurer Berdon agreed that the novelty was real. He said he'd support bringing on a test case as long as I drafted the legislation to come within the precedent of the *Roan* case. In doing this, it was a pleasure to have a prior practicing lawyer as treasurer, because he understood the legalese and related well to my expertise.

I explained to Berdon how we tested the use of state credit in Alaska in the *Suber* case and the procedure in filing such a case. (I described this in Chapter 13 of Volume 1.) Berdon gave me the name of the lawyer he knew from his private practice who would be the attorney of record to challenge the validity of the bonds and take care that the courts would have a legitimate case or controversy to decide.

This would not just be "opinion of justices" as in some states (e.g., Maine, Rhode Island) where bond counsel needed the court's assurances on a close call regarding the validity of the bond issues.

In those states, it was established that advisory opinions could be just that—advisory. That meant relying on that advice could never subject the bond counsel to negligence in approving a "close call." But such an opinion did not set a legal precedent because it was not rendered in an actual case of controversy. There was no technical defect or ethical issue in encouraging a taxpayer (albeit an employee in a law firm) as a resident citizen in the state from being encouraged to file as the plaintiff.

A taxpayer was found, followed by a complaint being filed and fully processed to the Supreme Court of Connecticut. I encouraged every aspect of a public purpose challenge to be included in the briefing and provided the attorney general's office with every conceivable defense and argument. That way, the decision of the court (one way or other) would not leave out any aspect of law, and it would be decided in all respects, valid or invalid. The court's decision was clear and unequivocal.

Today, the law in Connecticut is this: Under that public/private emoluments clause of the constitution, if the legislature clearly determined a proposed use of public monies was a proper public emolument (based on my draft, it clearly had), then the court would *not* substitute its judgment; it would defer to that finding, and the bonds would be validly issued.

What was the result? Our Hawkins opinion and the disclosure of the decision of the court allowed hundreds of millions of state general obligation bonds to be issued. The proceeds were deposited into the venture capital fund of that authority, today called Connecticut Innovations, Inc.

Directing the Investments

As a sequel, the board hired an astute attorney highly skilled in venture capital underwriting, from Skadden Arps as its executive director. For a number of years, the investments were wildly successful, returning in excess of 15 percent. It earned the executive money on his employment contract consistent with industry standard in annual amounts exceeding $1 million. Yet that proved to be too much politically for any state employee to earn! Consequently, he was terminated.

Times and opportunities have changed over the years, but the investments continue to be profitable (although nowhere as profitable as before). Now, many states have found similar ways and financial structures for investing taxpayer dollars in startup companies. Simply stated, the successes over the past by investing in venture capital products have been enough to warrant public monies for that purpose.

Fortunately, though, the private sectors as well as pension funds have been the primary investors, because it still is a "risky business."

CHAPTER 15

What's "In the State" versus "Of the State"?

This chapter provides insight into the relationship between the United States and the Indian Nations that are "within" but not a part of any state.

In 1976, a major matter in Maine—almost in the nature of a natural disaster—caused the credit market to close down on all Maine state and municipal bond issues. This fiscal credit crisis is best summarized as follows: Any tribe providing proof of being a continuously operating tribe could be recognized by federal law as a separate nation. Such a recognized nation, through litigation in Maine, was complicating all governmental and commercial transactions in every state where an Indian tribe was recognized. It was like the hand of God reaching down to punish the current generation for the sins of our forefathers.

What could each recognized Indian Nation claim? Each could demand that its land be returned to its rightful owners and each should be paid damages suffered by illegal seizure. This claim didn't apply to just any land. In Maine, for example, the recognized nation claimed the land of the entire city of Portland and more.

Doing Bond Business in Maine

First, let's discuss why Hawkins was doing bond business in Maine. After buying a summer home in Maine in 1968, Gerry Fernandez met several important politicians there. Bob Rosenberg[91] arrived at Hawkins in 1968 three years after me, and he and I had one of those lifelong productive, rewarding partnerships in which we split up our work and supported each other. During Rosenberg's freshman year at the firm, I had several special retainers with Connecticut, including drafting and creating the Connecticut Housing Finance Authority coupled with a novel state reserve fund bond credit enhancement. I was extremely busy there. Meanwhile, I was Gerry Fernandez's only associate for New York. When Maine's governor called Gerry to retain us to establish a state HFA, we naturally turned to Bob to be the primary associate. He would also model his work after what I was structuring in Connecticut.

Just a few years later, the attorney general and later governor with the state treasurer asked if we, as bond counsel, could research and render an opinion on the potential outcome of the Indian land claims. When the state of Maine checked with the rating agencies, they were told the bond investors would probably accept such an opinion rendered by a recognized bond counsel. Doing that would reopen the bond market.

Hawkins has an ingrained protocol called the "two partner" rule for rendering validity bond opinions. It called for at least two bond partners to be ready to sign any opinion out of the ordinary. I also insisted on having a favorable office-written memorandum at the ready, not only to protect the firm as proof of the reasonableness of rendering the opinion but also to look at any issue "six ways to Sunday," thus ensuring it was right.

But to render the opinion on the possible outcome of this property and damage claim of an Indian Nation to this massive amount of land was not within our municipal bond expertise. Appropriately, we turned to our marvelous litigation partner and, frankly, the prime reason that my parents had been comfortable with me joining this "white shoe" firm.

Hawkins had a partner named Clarence Fried, a Jewish man reputed to be a former rabbi. This established the fact that, at least for my parents, my religion would not prove to be a barrier at Hawkins, nor would I be the first Jewish partner. Remember, I was hired in the 1960s when most law firms, country clubs, and suburbs were divided into WASPS, Jewish, and Catholic—all white—without ever focusing on women and persons of color. As recently as 2016, it was still newsworthy that Cravath had made its first Asian woman partner and then announced another woman to become its first presiding partner.[92]

Clarence Fried and Franklin Wood, with Tom Dewey, had shared offices as young lawyers when they started their practices. When Franklin Wood was invited to join Hawkins, Delafield & Longfellow, he set a condition on his move by asking for a partnership for Clarence Fried as well.

By the 1960s, Fried was quite well established at Hawkins and respected as the partner in charge of litigation for the national broadcasting station WABC. However, it was a first for Clarence to work on municipal bond matters. Yet, it was clear to me, Fernandez, and Rosenberg (and others) that to render the opinion requested by Maine, the firm would not only need more than any two-partner rule, but also the support of the entire firm.

In his practice defending the major broadcasting company, Fried had expertise in constitutional-based issues affecting free speech, privacy, and confidentiality. He was clearly conservative, well regarded, and, of importance, a long-term member of the Management Committee and confidant of Franklin Wood. He also had at that time an associate whom he regarded as an excellent researcher, so Clarence took on the assignment. He understood the time constraint. Not only was there a hold on any new bond issues from the state of Maine or any of its municipalities, but pricing its outstanding municipal bonds was on hold, and trading was restricted as well.

Within the short period of a month, Clarence reported he had drawn his conclusion. The question then became more about *how* to write the opinion. That way, it would be acceptable to reopen the bond market and yet balanced enough to be recognized as substantive research leading to a credible conclusion of law and not, if you will, a "bought" opinion.

Bear in mind, Hawkins had just been through the highly respected and relied-upon market validity opinion on the MAC "bailout" NYC fiscal crisis issue, our so-called "billion-dollar" opinion (described in Chapter 1 of Volume 1). We had good reason to anticipate that the market for Maine bonds was preparing to reopen on our favorable opinion alone.

At the same time, we recognized the precedent. After all, Maine wasn't the only state in which an Indian Nation was seeking damages and return of native land. Other lawyers were working on the issue for other states. So it was not only the public finance lawyers but some big corporate firms that had vastly more associates engaged in research.

Hawkins concluded[93] that the claim for return of property would *not* be successful for a variety of technical reasons along the lines of adverse possession, laches, lack of title, etc. The claim for damages more than likely would be honored. However, the amount was not likely to be near current value, and payment would undoubtedly be shared by the state and the federal government—perhaps with greater amounts by the federal government.

Remember, this was a conclusion of law. I believe we also alluded (separately or when we made our opinion public) that to prevent this issue from becoming a fiscal crisis in other states, it would be best for the federal government to assume responsibility. Perhaps, it needed full liability to negotiate and settle with each nation. Alternatively, at the federal level, they could legislate a fair resolution that absolved the states of serious liability.

That opinion did reopen the Maine bond market and, in general, the federal government substantially covered the liability. No land was ordered to be returned. The research established that when in fact a tribe had signed such a treaty involving land, these tribes thought the transaction was transferring hunting rights to the land, because there was no concept of actual land ownership.

Patronizing Tradition

The legal treatment by the federal government of Native Americans (aka Indians) has a strained, paternalistic, patronizing tradition. The most obvious example is the Indian Gaming Act. It establishes a clear preference in law permitting casinos by an Indian tribe that can establish itself as a continuously active and *in situ* tribe; it is so certified by the Indian Gaming Board.

In U.S. law, such a tribe is a nation. Its land is *in but not of* any state. As a separate nation and in any state that has "gaming," a certified tribe is entitled to conduct casinos with poker, blackjack, and horse and game betting. Gaming is broadly defined, with church or temple bingo being included in the category. Bingo is a traditional American pastime, so in most states, because it permits forums for bingo, it must permit Indian casinos if tribes that are certified apply. This is true even if that state's constitution or statute bans casinos. California has such a constitutional provision, and Connecticut has such a statutory ban.

Second, no state or its municipalities or the federal government can impose taxes on the land or income of the nation or a member of the tribe ("member" is defined as anyone with 1/16'h parentage). As a result, when the Mohegan Tribe was certified as a continuous active tribe and established its Casino in Montville, Connecticut (between New London and Norwich where my grandparents had homes), friends of my deceased grandfather came to me. They suggested I check my lineage because perhaps the folklore about them coming over in the 1880s to avoid the pogroms in the Polish pale covered up my grandmother's native Indian roots.

Do Casinos Benefit the Community?

In my view, the culture of the Native Americans has not been enhanced or advanced by permitting gambling casinos nor has it been established that they benefit any community. Certainly, with leisure dollars being sucked into casinos, many communities lose attendance for movies, performing arts, and other local attractions.

Governor Lowell Weicker was adamantly opposed to having casino gambling in Connecticut. But once the chief of the Pequots clarified to him that the Pequot tribe was a separate nation and *not "in"* Connecticut, he relented, resulting in a negotiated memorandum of understanding.[94] The tribe agreed to pay the state a percentage of the "gross" from its gaming revenues.

The Pequot tribe was given the exclusive right to conduct casino gambling in Connecticut and on its land. Either the governor had not expected that another tribe could be certified in accordance with the technical requirements of the Indian Gaming Act (IGA), or he was trying to contractually block more casinos.

Regardless, the Mohegan tribe was persistent *and* had the backing of a wealthy former South African developer of resorts. After a number of years, the tribe was finally certified as a nation under the IGA.

At first, Governor Weicker insisted he could not and would not abrogate his "exclusive" contract with the Pequots, but the chief of the Mohegans suggested he talk to the chief of the Pequots. Governor

Weicker did that, and the Pequots chief told him that the Pequots and the Mohegans had been friendly for over three hundred years. The governor was "free" to talk to the Mohegans. Whatever that tribe and the governor worked out, the Pequots would go along with. In other words, the Pequots relinquished any right to be exclusive and without litigation or consideration, thus reflecting a principle in Indian culture among friendly tribes.

Of course, the Mohegans contracted for the same deal regarding the gross so both tribes would be co-exclusive.[95] From a pure business perspective, the two nations are located fewer than twenty miles apart. They're within a one- to three-hour drive from New York, Boston, and Hartford on interstate roads. For them, having two major casinos nearby is very attractive to gamblers who switch back and forth as their luck comes and goes. Both tribes apparently understood the business value of two competing nearby casinos. In fact, these two casinos have been successful, with new casinos now being planned elsewhere in Connecticut and Massachusetts.

Mohegans

In his work life, the chief of the Mohegans at the time was a sculptor of stone. He compared the path to being fully qualified under the Indian Gaming Act like working on a stone sculpture. By that, he explained that the last chip on the piece could cause the whole stone to splinter into multiple pieces. So, until he had that actual certification in hand, he had nothing. Any lack of proof could stop the whole process. Clearly, the Indian culture has patience, persistence, and persuasion as key principles.

The sequel to the Mohegan chapter of gaming is that the private developer of its hotel and casino had received a percentage of the gross for twenty-five years as well as a management contract as part of his fee. Subsequently, years later, the tribe determined it could manage its own affairs and renegotiated with the developer to terminate the management arrangements for a longer and bit larger percent of the gross.

Gaming at the time was a growth industry, but the developer determined that, rather than hold the notes of an enterprise it wasn't managing, it made sense to securitize its interest in future revenue from that renegotiated contract. Accordingly, the developer had a private placement to investors of notes payable at that percentage until the contract expired. Because of the discounted "present value" of the revenues to be collected, he received a substantial amount of money.

Since then, "gaming" has not done as well; the timing of getting out proved to be smart.

Pequots

For many years, before being certified under the Indian Gaming Act to open a casino, the Pequots operated a bingo establishment on its reservation. It attracted players from as far away as Buffalo, New York, because its payoffs were considerably higher than its church or temple competitors.

At one point before the Indian Gaming Act, the Pequot leaders decided to expand its bingo hall and hired Charles Klewin, a small contractor from Norwich, Connecticut. At the point of half completion, the economy declined. The tribe told Charlie to stop building because it had no money to pay him for any further work. Charlie told them he would complete the job on his own and hope for an upturn, so he could get paid. When it became certified to build the casino, the tribe returned that favor by having Charlie build out the entire casino facility and its entertainment facilities, making him an extremely wealthy person. No public bidding, just loyalty to Charlie.

Tribes and Taxation in California

Governor Arnold Schwarzenegger won the California election in 2003.[96] Hawkins was retained to solve one of his campaign promises—to create a financial structuring so that many Indian casinos operating in California would provide support to the state's general fund and help balance the budget, which was slipping into a serious deficit. The Indian Gaming Act did permit pass-through charges for road improvements, policing of errant drivers or robberies, and other similar enforcement expenses or regulatory requirements at the intersection of the nation and the state. But taxing the property and income on its profit from its casino was clearly not allowed.

So we came up with the concept of a "franchise fee" by which the state would authorize each tribe to have an exclusive franchise in the region of its tribal land. Our analysis was based on the "exclusive" precedents of Connecticut's two memos of understanding.

The "facts on the ground" fit almost perfectly. The tribes that had been qualified under the Indian Gaming Act in California were operating in various parts of the state in almost franchise-like, non-overlapping patterns. Tribal leaders explained to us (as the lawyers for the state) the legal reason for supporting payment of such a franchise fee. Here's what they said: While the California Constitution included a provision permitting only Indian nations to have casinos, the tribes understood that, in California, constitutional amendments happened regularly for political reasons. For example, the established "non-Indian emperors" of casinos in Las Vegas such as Steve Wynn could campaign to repeal such a provision, be successful, and then build casinos to compete with the tribes. But if the tribes had "contract" franchises with the state, then as long as that contract was in play and extendable, the federal contract clause under the U.S. Constitution "protected" the franchise from cancellation by the state.

The attorneys for the tribes believed it even provided permanent injunctive relief rather than just monetary damages. The irony, of course, is that law precluding contract impairment is explicitly part of the U.S. Constitution, while no Indian nation had such a reciprocal "constitutional" contract provision. (Remember, the nations are separate entities and are not bound by the U.S. Constitution as the California state government is bound.)

We were having a difficult time researching how to protect bondholders if a nation decided to "repudiate" its contract. We finally determined that the enormous economic incentives would have to suffice in our description of the enforcement mechanism in the offering document. In other words, the financial plan called for entering into a franchise, with each recognized tribe paying an annual franchise fee. Then those fees would be "securitized" to secure a bond issue. The proceeds of those bonds would help fund the current state general fund deficit.

Plan Challenged in Court

What we did not anticipate was a challenge from a certified Indian tribe, which claimed franchise grants like these were illegal under the Indian Gaming Act. The grants prevented a tribe from operating outside its own land. Since the statute did not preclude a second franchise being awarded if there was another tribe certified and seeking a permit for the same area, we had not anticipated any challenge from an Indian tribe.

But this tribe complained that the Indian Gaming Act restricted the power of the state from precluding an Indian nation expanding to any place in the state. Even more important, the tribe challenged exacting a franchise fee as a disguised "tax" that was prohibited by the Indian Gaming Act. As the case wound its way through the court, it precluded marketing any bonds as a securitization of the present value of those aggregated franchise fees. In fact, the last lower court to rule on the matter declared such a fee invalid. Thus, the state chose to abandon further appeals.

However, despite that lower court ruling, the Indian tribes and the state chose to honor the contract arrangements. Hence, the franchise fee program continues in California, and the general fund budget benefits annually. Each tribe with a franchise contract believes it has contractual protection of the ban on competition, even in the event the state constitutional provision is repealed or amended to allow non-Indian gambling casinos. While the securitization of the present value did not occur, the state still receives serious amounts of money annually, and the tribes gained contract security.

CHAPTER 16

What about Public Financing in Eastern Europe?

This chapter highlights the efforts taken to attract public finance business from Eastern European countries after the fall of the Berlin Wall.

With the end of the Cold War signaling a need to rebuild infrastructure in Eastern Europe, many public finance investment bankers were attracted to business opportunities there and in Russia. But unlike the aftermath of World War II, there would be no Marshall Plan for Eastern Europe. The financing task had been left to the private sector.

Some of my friends at prestigious corporate law and banking firms headed to Eastern Europe to propose various infrastructure financings, particularly for highways, hospitals, and other potential and recognized revenue-producing facilities. My firm didn't have the resources for the repeat visits necessary to persuade the Eastern Europe governmental proponents of our legal skills. That's especially true because we had to compete with large Wall Street corporate firms such as White & Case and Dewey Ballantine. They were opening offices, hiring European-educated lawyers, and taking on influential former U.S. State Department officials as partners.

However, we persuaded the Polish government (probably due to our low fee structure) of our legal skills in negotiating a long-term concession toll road and its coordinate financing. Europe had never had the benefit of a peaceful environment. There, much lending had been done by the banks and was short term. Our skill set in coordinating the allocation of risks and benefits based on thirty-year financing was critical to the parties accepting the concession agreement without acrimony. Although we had a three year retainer, we didn't make any money because of the number of trips needed, the dedication of a full-time partner, and the teaching time required. (People in these countries were credit neophytes.)

It became clear that unless Hawkins arranged to have an office and its staffing in one or more of the countries, we would be overextending ourselves trying to compete for that business. This would be detrimental to our ever-expanding business in California, Oregon, Connecticut, and elsewhere.

Was Doing Business in Eastern Europe Good for Us?

We did have one venture that proved, to me at least, that business in Eastern Europe was just not for us. Bob Rosenberg met one day with a Dr. Robert Cohen (as I recall his last name), who claimed to be qualified to practice medicine in the United States but had "connections" in his native Romania. We met with Robert C. several times, discussed projects, and talked with several Romanian emissaries with impressive-looking cards from financial firms we were unfamiliar with. Some of those officials were also part of the team from Romania working to get that country accepted into NATO.

Robert C was convinced that his governmental connections and our expertise in coordinating and counseling on public infrastructure matched the financing counsel needs of his country. Plus he claimed he'd arrange for us to meet with his country's president—as long as we developed a serious proposal that would appeal to him. With that, he convinced us to pay for our travel to Romania.

Based on our research, we had developed at least two viable projects respecting two infrastructures that were needed and might generate revenues sufficient to access the world bond market. Robert C.'s pitch was that Romania was being shut out of the worldwide markets (reasons discussed below), and creative financial structuring lawyers could figure out how to bring Romania back into the bond market—properly. For some reason, he had decided Bob and our firm was perfect for this role and we had concluded that "nothing ventured, nothing gained."

Cordoba is on the Black Sea. During the Cold War, President Nicolae Ceauşescu had built a canal from that port to the Danube in Hungary. This way, ships from Israel, Turkey, Georgia, and other countries on or near the Black Sea could transport their goods through the Black Sea. They could then transfer those goods at Cordoba to barges and travel through the canal directly to the middle of Europe.

In addition, Cordoba needed a new expanded highway to the capital city of Bucharest. Why? Because the Roma, a significant minority in Romania, impeded the traffic with their wagons. The thought was to let the Roma use the old road, thus allowing the trucking and car traffic to speed along a new toll road.

We determined the best strategy would be to offer each of the countries bordering the Black Sea discounted passage through the canal in consideration of each commitment to use the port and set up their landing spaces and offices. (This would be like the original planning of nineteenth-century Shanghai.) We were forced to consider creditworthy partners, because former President Ceauşescu had made a major miscalculation due to his misunderstanding of how world credit markets work. That is, he had paid off all Romanian debt to the point that no banks had a vested economic interest in

Romania.[97] He also drained the government's coffers by building a golden palace capital building.

The feasibility of developing the port was based on our experience in waste-to-energy financing where many municipalities contracted to put their solid waste into a waste-to-energy facility. The "credit" of those municipalities to pay for that disposal service was the security for the bond issues.

Supportive Partners

After studying the Black Sea map, it was clear that Russia, Georgia, Turkey, and even Israel could be supportive partners. Bringing their goods to this port and then shipping them on through the canal to the rest of Europe would be cost effective. Therefore, getting use guarantees for port use was expected to be easy if we had the right bankers and the right connections. The negotiations would be fascinating, and for Romania, it would be huge for employment and prestige. Goods would be coming the other way from Europe through the Danube and the canal, and then returning to those countries. That meant the coordination and economics of scale would be assured, and markets would increase as a result.

The economics of this project were developed by financial friends from the New York municipal office of investment banks. There seemed to be a genuine interest, particularly with the road first and then the contract concessions with the other countries. Dr. Robert Cohen, we also learned, had strong ties to other Romanian leaders because he'd been a key player in arranging for Jews leaving Russia to pass through Romania on their way to Israel.[98] As we would later learn, connections were important, but currency was critical.

Presenting Our Plan

Three of us flew to Bucharest, Romania's capital, and were met at the airport by a contingency of governmental officials. Each was driven in a Mercedes by a bulky driver who was "carrying." We were escorted to a campus-like former Russian military building built to withstand bombing. There, we prepared for our meeting with the president. The time was set for an hour before President Ceauşescu was to speak with the NATO alliance requesting that Romania be admitted. Not only did we meet with the president and six key staff members, but he discussed our two projects and extended our interview another hour, delaying his speech to NATO delegates. Not only was he enthusiastic, but he told his "friend Robert" he had fond memories of all the good work Dr. Cohen had done for Israel and Romania. He said he thought ships coming up from Israel would be symbolic of Romania's successful transition, and that he would leave it to Dr. Cohen and his staff to work out the details. What a fine meeting with the president of Romania.

We returned to our Hawkins partners to report on this successful meeting. We even thought we'd have the retainer without a competitive process. We also thought Robert was the right contact and we had proposed the right projects.

Weeks went by. Slowly but surely, we realized the deal we thought we had struck wouldn't be easy and probably wouldn't happen. President Ceauşescu was running for reelection and needed political contributions. Dr. Cohen finally came clean and made it clear the number the president had in mind as our "contribution" for our project was well above our pay grade. Not only that, we were of the opinion that such a payment could be contrary to American laws that prevented this sort of economic incentive—bribery by its popular name. Not achieving leverage through political payoff denied us the retainer in the end.

Banking in Hungary

On a more positive note was my business trip to Hungary to conduct a seminar with Eastern European investment bankers and banking counsel on housing and project mortgage financing. None of the citizens of Eastern European countries had experienced private ownership of land or had even incurred personal debt. There, the government provided the housing and public water and sewer systems, allocating where people lived. Their standard of living depended on their commitment to the party. Similarly, the municipalities within the Communist countries did not do any bonding for infrastructure.

We were at the Offit Bank, which was then specializing in loans to governments. Our seminar was intended to describe how the bank's personnel could leverage their assets by selling collateralized mortgages. We soon learned that their governmental infrastructure loans were short term, because the banks were simply not yet long-term lenders. The instability in Europe during the early twentieth century resulting from wars between sovereign states had basically precluded long-term bonding by municipalities, even in Western Europe.

However, one banker told us what he was doing: In Hungary, all the former Russian military bases (of which there were many throughout that country) became the property of the municipality in which the base was situated. The constitution permitted municipalities to mortgage or sell "excess properties" and, for the most part, there was no current municipal need for these military bases. They were easily tagged "excess property."

This Offit banker was lending money to each of these communities for constructing water, sewer, and drainage facilities and accepting as collateral the "excess property" under a secured transaction. I called that Investment Banking 101.

Suffice it to say that Hawkins never developed any business in Europe. In fact, we were naïve to think that, without a high commitment of resources, our expertise was enough.

ABOUT THE AUTHOR

Richard Land Sigal practiced public finance from 1964 to 2016, including fifty years with the national law firm of Hawkins Delafield & Wood. He was the bond counsel or underwriters' partner in charge of major tax exempt or taxable bond issues in many states as well as the Commonwealth of Puerto Rico. A graduate of Yale University (1960) and the University of Chicago School of Law (1963), Sigal's contribution to the creation of financing strategies to support the growth of public infrastructure are unmatched.

- During his career, Sigal crafted innovative, precedent-setting public finance structures, including:
- First Clean Water Bond program that leveraged federal water and sewer grants
- First revenue bonds secured by state income or sales tax that restructured New York City debt in 1975, funded the multi-billion-dollar New York State Spring borrowing in 1983, and first securitization of those revenues to finance each of New York City's and New York State's new capital programs
- First bond securitization of the annual in-perpetuity payments of the major tobacco companies to states and the counties in New York and California to fund major infrastructure programs
- First public-private partnerships to finance waste-to-energy plants based on put-or-pay delivery contracts of municipalities to private corporations with patented technology
- First state "first-time homebuyer" and low- and moderate-housing finance general bond resolution (not project-by-project financings)

- First state venture capital finance program
- First statewide program to acquire development rights of farmland
- First multiyear, multibillion-dollar program to modernize a state's flagship university
- First tax-exempt bond programs to finance new sources of power or to stabilize existing power authorities secured by statutorily mandated utility charges

Among his most significant contributions was developing a special tax in 2006 to secure a multibillion-dollar bond issue to fund general fund deficits of the Commonwealth of Puerto Rico. That security structure withstood a challenge in 2019 during the recent Puerto Rico bankruptcy. It is expected to be used as a prime structure to finance the many new capital needs of that territory.

Mr. Sigal was a two-year chairman of the New York State Bar Association—Municipal Law Section, chairman of Bond Buyer National Conferences held in San Francisco and New York and received the Corporate Affiliate Award in 2008 for outstanding service to the profession and the National Association of State Treasurers.

Mr. Sigal resides in New York City with his wife Samayla Deutch, who is also an attorney.

Visit his web site at: RichardLandSigal.com

ACKNOWLEDGMENTS

I'm grateful for the assistance of Deirdre Roney, Esq. in tracking down references and clarifying my sentences. I also appreciate the encouragement and assistance from Laurie Schwartz, Esq. Both lawyers are former associates who contributed to the bond issue case studies described in this book. I am also grateful for the Dudley Court Press team who made both volumes of this work come to life.

—Richard Land Sigal

APPENDIX A

[*Washington Post* article on Nixon/Mudge Rose related to bond business. Find the full article at WashingtonPost.com]

JACK ANDERSON ON THE WASHINGTON MERRY-GO-ROUND

President Nixon's Old Law Firm Doing Very Well in the Capital

When there's loose money lying around in Washington, President Nixon's old law firm increasingly is available to help pick it up.

Take, for instance, the proposed $2.55 billion Washington subway, which had become side-tracked until the former Nixon firm got busy behind the scenes.

No one would suggest that Mudge, Rose, Guthrie and Alexander is going to get all $2.55 billion simply because President Nixon is in the White House and another former partner, John Mitchell, is Attorney General. So far the old Nixon firm has a grip only on about $200,000.

The subway is being financed in part with an $880 million bond float, and the lawyers who handle such floats are always sure of rich profits.

While the subway was in its dreaming stages, from 1966 to 1969, the New York firm of Hawkins, Delafield and Wood did a highly acceptable job of working up plans for the bond issues. But the big money was still to come.

Last June, the Hawkins, Delafied firm found out what kind of league they were playing in. Their bond man, Robert Ferdon, who was working on the Washington bond deal, jumped over to the law firm of Mudge, Rose. Mitchell had been the firm's top municipal bond attorney, and someone unquestionably was needed to step into his shoes.

Behind closed doors, partner Frank Wood of Hawkins, Delafield and Wood fought to keep the Washington Metropolitan Area Transit Authority as a client, citing the firm's long service.

A memorandum of the meeting prepared by WMATA's general manager, Jackson Graham, states that Wood and his colleagues "were, of course, anxious to retain the Authority as a client."

But the memo, obtained by this column, ended with the story of Wood's defeat. The WMATA general manager recommended that a switch be made to Mudge, Rose. The move was officially ratified June 30.

Sudden Solutions

By an amazing coincidence, the Nixon Administration and the Washington, D.C., government, both subject to the President, swiftly began to break the logjams that had blocked the much-needed subway.

As Mudge, Rose began to work on the bond issues— which will enrich the firm a minimum of $200,000 in the next eight to ten years— the voices of discord became voices of harmony.

The city government yielded a bit to the freeway backers who had previously thwarted the subway. The congressional subcommittees also responded. After wrangling years of disagreement, the President was able to sign and announce a $1.15 billion authorization on December 9, only five months after his old law firm had been cut into the subway deal.

The "Metro" promises to be a beauty. Its 98 miles will serve both the suburbs and the inner city. No one questions its need.

Robert Ferdon explained to this column that he and the President's old law partners were "brought together by some friends." The WMATA said that Ferdon's know-how "was important enough for us to follow the man rather than the firm."

So everybody is happy. Except Hawkins, Delafield and Wood.

APPENDIX B

The Limits of Property Rights

June 24, 2005

The Supreme Court's ruling yesterday that the economically troubled city of New London, Conn., can use its power of eminent domain to spur development was a welcome vindication of cities' ability to act in the public interest. It also is a setback to the "property rights" movement, which is trying to block government from imposing reasonable zoning and environmental regulations. Still, the dissenters provided a useful reminder that eminent domain must not be used for purely private gain.

The city of New London has fallen on hard times. In 1998—when its population was at its lowest since 1920, and its unemployment rate was nearly twice the state average—an effort was begun to turn New London around. State and local officials put together a redevelopment plan, anchored by a $300 million Pfizer research center, that would bring restaurants, stores and a new Coast Guard museum to one hard-hit neighborhood.

The city authorized a nonprofit development corporation to clear the necessary land by eminent domain, a forced sale in which the seller is given appropriate compensation. The development corporation got control of most of the land it needed, but a few people refused to sell.

Eminent domain allows governments to take property for a public use, such as building a road. The property owners in New London claimed that handing over private property to a private developer cannot be a public use, even if it is part of a comprehensive plan to turn around a depressed city.

The Supreme Court, by a 5-to-4 vote, sided with the city. The court noted that in past cases it had taken a broad view on this issue and given governments wide discretion to determine when a taking of property meets this standard. New London, the court held, was within its rights to decide that its development plan was a valid public use. (*The New York Times* benefited from eminent domain in clearing the land for the new building it is constructing opposite the Port Authority Bus Terminal.)

In a blistering dissent, Justice Sandra Day O'Connor lamented that the decision meant that the government could transfer any private property from the owner to another person with more political influence "so long as it might be upgraded." That is a serious concern, but her fears are exaggerated. The majority strongly suggested that eminent domain should be part of a comprehensive plan, and Justice Anthony Kennedy, writing separately, underscored that its goal cannot simply be to help a developer or other private party become richer.

That is not the situation in New London. Connecticut is a rich state with poor cities, which must do everything they can to attract business and industry. New London's development plan may hurt a few small property owners, who will, in any case, be fully compensated. But many more residents are likely to benefit if the city can shore up its tax base and attract badly needed jobs.

https://www.nytimes.com/2005/06/24/opinion/the-limits-of-property-rights.html

APPENDIX C

Free Passage

When the George Washington Bridge and other bridges crossing the Hudson River were built, the construction money was raised by bond issues. They were issued under bond indentures that pledged the tolls as security for paying back the bonds. That also included covenants (contracts) with bondholders agreeing there would be no free passage except for emergency vehicles.

Years passed, and tolls were paid by drivers in both directions. But based on a need to prevent congestion, the question was asked: "Could one way be free of tolls?" As bond counsel for every authority that crossed the Hudson (including those upstate with similar "no free passage" covenants), the partners at Hawkins said, "Yes. Tolls could be charged one way at twice the price pursuant to the 'legal' fiction that the driver was paying once for passage both ways."

Then a related one-way tolls question arose for the George Washington Bridge. "Should we charge drivers going out from the city or coming back into the city?" The engineers smartly concluded there was plenty of open highway to permit backed-up traffic and have drivers pay coming into the city, rather than having the west side highway backed up into the local streets on the way out. Today, of course, electronic tolling makes this issue academic. Tollbooths have become archaic, but money collection still continues for two-way passage.

Locating Tollbooths

In Connecticut, the tollbooths were built on the road, while on the New York Thruway and other freeways, the tollbooths were constructed on the ingress and egress roads. This was due to a condition for approving the financing for the Connecticut Expressway. Legislators from Fairfield County, the richest county in the nation at the time, insisted on free passage in certain places, such as between Greenwich and Stamford. That required placing the tollbooths directly on the highway. As traffic increased on that road, the pollution and accidents directly resulting from the location of tollbooths caused the governor to remove tollbooths altogether and permit free use of the Connecticut turnpike.

Highway Tolls as a Source of State Revenue

Today, with electronic tolling, overhead cameras allow the state of Connecticut to raise revenues through tolls. Drivers can speed along without concern about congestion or reduced accidents caused by on-road tollbooths. That should mean reinstating tolling. Yet passing the law for that major revenue resource option has stalled for political reasons, despite the state's bond rating being reduced recently from its triple-A status. Moreover, the state could upwardly adjust the pricing for congested times of the day, thus discouraging nonessential driving during those hours.

The technology and business of adjusting tolls to curb congestion exists, but it seems that Connecticut—the land of steady habits—cannot adapt to this smart business approach. This is despite recent cases upholding commuter discounts as not being in violation of the Interstate Commerce Act. In addition, truck traffic can be precluded from diverting to local roads, and proper pricing can induce truckers to travel at other than commuter hours.

In the past, Connecticut usually had bipartisan support if a program was designed to maintain the state's triple-A rating (such as the UConn 2000 program discussed in Chapter 8 of Volume 1). Like elsewhere, Democrats claimed Republican opposition to reinstating concession price tolling on its interstates, despite a continuing decline in the state's rating and an almost desperate need for an additional revenue source besides the gas tax to pay for road maintenance. Even a proposal to achieve an enormous amount of money by awarding a sixty-year concession to a public/private partnership with a consortium of pension funds as happened successfully, respecting the Indiana turnpike has not gained Republican support. (See discussion on Chapter 6 in Volume 1.)

APPENDIX D

In New York, the state's constitution required any issuance of bonds to be approved by a majority vote in a statewide referendum to secure those bonds according to the "faith and credit" pledge of the state government—that is, to pay the debt service from any and all taxes. Going the referendum route, New York Governor Rockefeller had failed twice to accomplish this during the 1960s. Next, Governor Rockefeller, with the advice of bond lawyer John Mitchell, then proposed an approach to create a separate authority. The state legislature created the Housing Finance Authority (HFA), and gave HFA the power to issue revenue bonds to finance multifamily rental housing projects for low- and moderate-income families. These revenue bonds would be secured by the rents and enhanced by the "moral obligation" as described below.

Here's the background to the concept of establishing authorities. In the 1930s, Robert Moses created what became the legal way to circumvent the referendum restriction noted above. His solution was to form a separate authority to issue revenue bonds, including bonds to finance the Long Island Expressway, the Triborough Bridge and Tunnel, the power facilities at Niagara Falls, and the Southern State Parkway.[99] However, each of these bond issues was secured by revenues and marketed with feasibility studies, which supported that source as being sufficient to pay the bonds (self-liquidation). When it came to bond issues for housing projects, though, feasibility consultants claimed that rentals from low- and mid-income people could not be counted on. To attract investors and market the bonds, John Mitchell concocted what became known as the "moral obligation."[100] This required the FHA's chairman to certify the need for an annual contribution from the state that would supplement rental income and ensure payment of bond debt service.

This certification process did not obligate the state to appropriate the necessary funds; that would have created an unconstitutional debt obligation. Yet, the market expected the state government to honor the request as its "moral obligation." In other words, if the legislation were drafted as a legal obligation to appropriate and pay the amount certified, it would be debt. And because it was not approved at a referendum, it would be unconstitutional.

This process describes how "moral obligation" debt became the door that opened the state government to finance projects through its Urban Development Corporation to include housing for all income levels such as found on Roosevelt Island.[101]

A Moral Obligation Backing

The Urban Development Corporation in New York was created in 1975. Its legislation also included a "moral obligation" reserve fund feature, but it did not include any requirement (at least embedded in the statute) of a finding of selfsufficiency.[102]

One of the members of that board told me that when the approval of the housing for Roosevelt Island was being presented, the financial advisors had expressed serious concerns about whether the rent levels could raise enough money to pay debt service on the UDC bonds. The staff then alluded to a theory used by previous boards that passed on projects deemed "shaky" financially. It was fail/crash. That meant the board had no statutory requirement to determine self-sufficiency and accordingly, acted on this theory: If the state "failed to appropriate" debt service, the New York bond market would "crash." In 1975, it was the default on notes of UDC that triggered NYC's fiscal crisis. That means the moral obligation in New York was being treated as a state guarantee to pay the debt as the trade-off to getting the necessary housing development built and financed.

ENDNOTES

[1] Predatory price was the allegation. It involved violating the antitrust rules in that the IOU was purposely lowering its price serving next door to those customers of the Municipal Light Company to entice them to switch to service of the IOU.

[2] "The Cleveland banking community apparently was making a deliberate effort to unseat maverick Mayor Dennis Kucinich when it forced that city into financial default by failing to refinance $14 million in municipal notes, according to a House Banking subcommittee staff report." Larry Kramer, "Cleveland Default Linked to Effort To Unseat Mayor," *Washington Post, July 17, 1979, https://www.washingtonpost.com/archive/politics/1979/07/17/cleveland-default-linked-to-effort-to-unseat-mayor/e7415b31-282d-4df1-8bc5-9d3e0e2c0acb/?noredirect=on&utm_term=.1cc115382e51.*

[3] Case Western Reserve Univ., "Encyclopedia of Cleveland History: Squire, Sanders and Dempsey," *https://case.edu/ech/articles/s/squire-sanders-and-dempsey.*

[4] "Fiscal default, a term generally used to describe the point at which a city fails to pay fixed debts on loans or bonds on time . . . does not necessarily mean that bankruptcy is imminent . . . Although many of those who filled the stately, well-appointed council chambers last night exhibited shock and dismay at the fact that Cleveland now becomes the first major American city to default since the Depression, the prospects for this happening had been gelling for several weeks." Reginald Stuart, "City of Cleveland Defaults on Loans," *N.Y. Times*, December 16, 1978, *https://nyti.ms/1LYCcCd.* Devon-Ritchie, "Cleveland, Ohio defaults on $14,000,000 in loans, making it the first post-depression era city to do so," *Famous Daily, http://www.famousdaily.com/history/cleveland-defaults-on-loans.html.*

[5] My first introduction was a lunch hosted by executives of Edison Institute requesting my support for the container equipment protecting the nuclear power plants to be considered "air pollution control" equipment. I explained that I regarded this as mandated safety equipment, and we would require an IRS ruling on its treatment for tax-exempt bonds before we could opine. The Edison Institute tried to convince other bond firms of this approach, but finally dropped the matter.

[6] "'We can't become a state that stands like an ostrich with our head in the sand while our sister states become competitive,' Representative Moira K. Lyons, the House Democratic Majority Leader, said, adding that with the third-highest rates in the nation, Connecticut could only benefit from deregulation. Still, many states have balked at passing such legislation, and the Connecticut bill met resistance from some lawmakers who said they felt it included too many handouts to the state's two electric utilities, Northeast Utilities and United Illuminating." Jonathon Rabinovitz, "Connecticut Lawmakers Approve Electric Deregulation," *N.Y. Times April 16, 1998, https://www.nytimes.com/1998/04/16/nyregion/connecticut-lawmakers-approve-electric-deregulation.html.*

[7] One was the former Senate majority leader, William D. Bella, sanctioned in the Sylvester scandal, and one was the former counsel to the Speaker of the House.

[8] It is noted that my firm Hawkins Delafield is a boutique firm devoted solely to public finance, whereas the other top five firms doing this work are multipurpose law firms mostly dominated by the corporate practice, including long-standing relationships with the IOUs.

[9] TIF, or Tax-Increment-Financing, "is a public financing method that is used to incentivize and catalyze development, infrastructure, and other projects. Essentially, it allocates the future property tax revenues from a project or project area—that are above and beyond what would have been generated without project—to costs associated with the project. In other words, the property tax benefits from the project are used to help finance the project." "Connecticut Overhauls Tax-Increment-Financing (TIF): New Legislation Opens the Door to More TIF Projects," Camoin Associates, Economic Development, October 1, 2015, *https://www.camoinassociates.com/connecticut-overhauls-tax-increment-financing-tif-new-legislation-opens-door-more-tif-projects.*

"Tax-increment financing (TIF) is an increasingly popular way for cities to promote economic development." Randal O'Toole, "Crony Capitalism and Social Engineering, The Case against Tax-Increment Financing," CATO Institute, May 18, 2011, *https://object.cato.org/pubs/pas/PA676.pdf.*

[10] "Groton, the Connecticut city first considered, was ruled out, because it lacked an adequate stadium site, and the financing there was uncertain. Then Norwich was selected, despite a last-ditch effort by Mario M. Cuomo,

then New York's Governor, to keep the Yankees in Albany, where they had been for 12 years." Jack Cavanaugh, "How a Yankees Farm Team, Newly Named, Landed in Norwich," *N.Y. Times, March 26, 1995, https://www.nytimes.com/1995/03/26/nyregion/how-a-yankees-farm-team-newly-named-landed-in-norwich.html.*

[11] Marc Santora, "51 Months For Key Figure In Corruption," *N.Y. Times, November 21, 2003, https://www.nytimes.com/2003/11/21/nyregion/51-months-for-key-figure-in-corruption.html.*

[12] "Looking the part of the button-down financial watchdog in a black suit, a white shirt, striped tie and round wire-rimmed glasses, Mr. Hevesi, 70, said in State Supreme Court in Manhattan that he had approved a $250 million pension investment in exchange for nearly $1 million in benefits from a California businessman, Elliott Broidy." Danny Hakim and William Rashbaum, "Hevesi Pleads Guilty in Pension Case," *N.Y. Times*, October 7, 2010, *https://www.nytimes.com/2010/10/08/nyregion/08hevesi.html*

[13] "Lisa A. Thiesfield, who claims she spent all of the $1.1 million she was paid by an investment firm that bribed her married boyfriend, the corrupt former state treasurer Paul Silvester, was ordered Tuesday to serve six months in jail and pay a $50,000 fine." Don Michak, "Silvester's Mistress Gets 6 Months in Jail," *Journal Inquirer, March 3, 2004, http://www.journalinquirer.com/archives/silvester-s-mistress-gets-months-in-jail/article_2881cbf6-814a-5020-9994-bb89b7a4884a.html*

[14] Court Orders William DiBella, Former Majority Leader of the Connecticut State Senate, to Pay Over $791,000 in Connection with Fraud Relating to State Pension Fund. "The Securities and Exchange Commission announced today that on March 13, 2008, the Honorable Ellen Bree Burns, United States District Judge for the District of Connecticut, entered a judgment imposing sanctions against William A. DiBella, the former Majority Leader of the Connecticut State Senate, and his consulting firm, North Cove Ventures, L.L.C. for their roles in aiding and abetting then Treasurer of the State of Connecticut, Paul J. Silvester in a fraudulent investment scheme. Pursuant to the scheme, Silvester had invested $75 million in state pension funds with Thayer Capital Partners, a Washington, DC-based private equity firm, and arranged for Thayer to pay DiBella a percentage of the investment, though he did not do work to justify the payment." Securities And Exchange Commission. Litigation Release No. 20498, March 14, 2008. *SEC v.*

William A. DiBella, et al, Civil Action No. 3:04 CV 1342 (EBB) (D. Conn.), https://www.sec.gov/litigation/litreleases/2008/lr20498.html.

[15] Most investment banking firms have internal funds available to pay for the bonds and then resell them over time to its wealthy customers.

[16] "Prosecutors alleged that Goldberg's firm, Matthews & Wright, had used NAFCU in a scheme that was apparently designed to create the false impression that over $2 billion in municipal bonds had been issued in time to beat restrictive provisions in the tax code. According to prosecutors, Matthews & Wright, trying to make it look like it had raised money for the bond issues, wrote bogus checks for hundreds of millions of dollars on a NAFCU account. They then claimed to deposit the checks in an offshore bank on the West Pacific island of Saipan. But the bank was nothing more than a shell (on many documents its mailing address was actually listed as CASE's headquarters)." Hella Winston, "They Made It Out of Gay," Tablet, *https://www.tabletmag.com/jewish-life-and-religion/192880/they-made-it-out-of-gay.* See also IMO ARTHUR ABBA GOLDBERG, An Attorney at Law, No. D-146, (Sup. Ct. NJ), November 9, 1995, *https://law.justia.com/cases/new-jersey/supreme-court/1995/d-146-94-opn.html.*

[17] "In 2004, Rowland resigned from office during a corruption investigation, and later pleaded guilty in federal court to a one-count indictment for conspiracy to commit honest services fraud, mail fraud and tax fraud . . . On April 10, 2014, Rowland was indicted on seven counts for his role in an election fraud case where former congressional candidate Lisa Wilson-Foley, current Vice Chair of the Bushnell Center for the Performing Arts and her husband, Brian Foley, pleaded guilty in federal court on March 31, 2014 to illegally paying Rowland $35,000 in campaign consulting fees. He was charged with two counts of falsifying records in a federal investigation, one count of conspiracy, two counts of causing false statements to be made to the FEC, and two counts of causing illegal campaign contributions. He was convicted on all seven counts in September 2014 and was subsequently sentenced to 30 months in prison on March 18, 2015." Wikipedia, "John Rowland," accessed July 14, 2018, *https://en.wikipedia.org/wiki/John_G._Rowland.* See also Matthew Ormseth, "John Rowland, Former Governor Convicted Of Corruption And Fraud, Released From Custody," *Hartford Courant, May 27, 2018.*

[18] "When Governor Rowland took office in 1995, his message was loud and clear: Connecticut's new governor doubled the State Commission on the Arts' budget. It was a matter of dollars and common sense, he said—with an economic impact of $1.3 billion and support of 30,000 jobs, the nonprofit arts sector deserved a larger public investment. Governor Rowland's extraordinary commitment over the past five years has catapulted Connecticut from the bottom 10% in per capita state arts support to #1 in the continental United States. Today, the State arts appropriation exceeds $13.5 million.

"In addition to increasing program funds for the arts, Governor Rowland has authorized more than $54 million in capital fund investments in the state's arts infrastructure. Projects are underway today in communities across the state, ranging from the restoration of long dormant, historic theaters, to the transformation of old factory buildings into arts centers and housing for artists, to the construction of major new performing arts venues. The Governor has also made a commitment to increase the Connecticut Arts Endowment Fund by $1 million annually. The Fund, which helps stabilize Connecticut's art industry by rewarding organizations that demonstrate an increased ability to raise funds from the private sector, stands at $14 million, with a goal of $20 million. Furthermore, the State's Art-in-Public Spaces program has a current authorization of more than $6 million for public art projects." Americans for the Arts, "Governor John G. Rowland," 2001, *https://www.americansforthearts.org/by-program/promotion-and-recognition/awards-for-arts-achievement/annual-awards/public-leadership-in-the-arts/gov-john-g-rowland-r-ct.*

[19] "The Committee called their new non-profit organization, The Greater New York Association, later renamed The New York Racing Association (NYRA). Chartered on April 28, 1955, the Association counted on the strong backing of New York Governor W. Averell Harriman, who in his 30s had owned a successful racing stable, Arden Farms, before turning to a career in government. The New York State Legislature complied, and in June 1955 granted NYRA a 25-year franchise grant that guaranteed it a minimum 4 percent of pari-mutuel handle at downstate tracks and 5 percent at Saratoga to be used for capital improvements." The New York Racing Association: A Short History, *https://www.nyrainc.com/uploads/wysiwyg/assets/uploads/NYRA_A_Short_History_PROOF.pdf.*

[20] Louis Lefkowitz issued an opinion whereby he recognized that NYRA owned the land and that its incorporation papers did not require it to be

used as a racing land. Louis Lefkowitz served as attorney general for 22 years and no "attorney general before or since has had the impact that Louie Lefkowitz had." Nick Ravo, "Louis Lefkowitz, 22- Year Attorney General, Dies at 91" *N.Y. Times,* June 22, 1996, *https://www.nytimes.com/1996/06/22/nyregion/louis-lefkowitz-22-year-attorney-general-dies-at-91.html.*

[21] The professional group working on proposed legislation met several times at the plush offices of NYRA at the Belmont track. Before the meeting, usually commencing with lunch, each of us bought our tickets for the afternoon races, which were telecasts in the conference room. After each race, there was a pause in the conference so each of us could consult our ticket for the race to ascertain whether we had a winner. The windows were open after the meeting for us to present and collect on our winning ticket, if any.

[22] In other words, it was determined not to create an authority to bond and finance the improvements to Belmont. The state made what is termed "first instance loans" and once all major improvements were made from those loans, the state forgave repayment and received title to the land.

[23] Jack Anderson, "Nixon's Old Law Firm Doing Very Well," *Washington Post, February 16, 1976.*

[24] Ferdon's name was later added to the firm's name, but when the Nebraska and Salt River nuclear plants were built and fully financed, his municipal finance profits fell considerably. The firm itself fell apart; it had never become a firm with major corporate clients.

[25] "In December of 2000—energized, perhaps, by a major donation estimated by some sources to be in excess of $500,000—the Institute for Justice returned to New London. There they found seven people who had all previously stated that they were willing to sell their properties for varying but always large amounts of cash, now willing to say that what they really wanted was, at all costs, to remain in their houses. Since no one, except N.L.D.C., had seen fit to try and determine from the outset what these individuals really wanted, there was no one around now, other than N.L.D.C. to challenge their sudden change of heart—and that wasn't sufficient for our local newspaper."Ariston, "A Bright Shining Lie" presented orally by Stephen Percy, December 5, 2006. (The wording came from the typed speech, which I received for use in this book.)

[26] For the best analysis of this case and criticism of this professor's academic preferences, see: Robert C. Ellickson, *"Federalism and Kelo: A Question for Richard Epstein," Tulsa Law Review, http://ssrn.com/abstract=1418671.*

[27] *Kelo v. City of New London, 545 U.S. 469 (2005).*

[29] *Berman v. Parker,* 348 U.S. 26, (1954).

[29] "[Berman owns] property in Area B at 712 Fourth Street SW. It is not used as a dwelling or place of habitation. A department store is located on it. [Berman] object[s] to the appropriation of this property for the purposes of the project. They claim that their property may not be taken constitutionally for this project. It is commercial, not residential property; it is not slum housing; it will be put into the project under the management of a private, not a public, agency and redeveloped for private, not public, use." *Berman v. Parker,* 348 U.S. 26, 31 (1954).=, *http://cdn.loc.gov/service/ll/usrep/usrep348/usrep348026/usrep348026.pdf.*

"Berman, owned a department store located in the boundaries of the development plan. His store was not in disrepair, and it provided a service to the community in terms of employment and economy." Kenneth Poortvliet, "Berman v. Parker: Summary & Ruling," Study.com, *https://study.com/academy/lesson/berman-v-parker-summary-ruling.html.*

[30] Timothy S Hollister, "Who cares what the pundits think of Kelo?" *Connecticut Law Review* 48 (July 2016), 1463.

[31] Hearing on "The State of Property Rights in America Ten Years After *Kelo v. City of New London,* July 9, 2015, *http://www-assets.vermontlaw.edu/Assets/directories/FacultyDocuments/Echeverria_2015HouseTestimony.pdf*

[32] The best summary can be found by reading a speech delivered at a private event by an insider who thought that *The Day* handled the situation poorly. Here are the words of Stephen Percy: "Despite having factual evidence, the local media, and particularly The Day, continually ignored those facts, reported only one side of the debate on and use of eminent domain and totally failed in making any effort to determine all of the facts as events unfolded.

"After approximately three years of operation—and thanks to a grant from Fannie Mae—NLDC had its progress audited by a consulting firm called LISK—a process that lasted three days and involved interviews on their part with people all over the city. At the conclusion of their exit interview, the head of the firm made the following comment: 'You will not find this comment in our final report, but we feel obligated to make it to you— We have performed this audit function for over 1,500 economic development corporations throughout the United States. Of all those we evaluated, you are the only one who does not have the support of your local newspaper.'

"During the entire period from February 3rd of 1998 until [2006], no member of The Day Publishing Company from the editor and publishers to the editor and staff of the Editorial page to the editor of the News section—in other words, the majority of the policy makers on the paper—has ever tried, or directed a reporter to try, to get the NLDC's side of the story before publishing, unchallenged, what the property owners have had to say. They have not talked to Dave Goebel, our Chief Operating Officer from November of 1998 until his 'retirement' in November of 2005, Jim Mahoney, Jim Dunn, myself, Jane Walsh, or anyone also involved in the property acquisition process. When the current editor and publisher of the paper directed Morgan McGinley to call me approximately a year ago, Morgan explained why he hadn't contacted me by saying, 'Well, Steve, I know how you felt.' In spite of this lack of contact, *The Day* has frequently and continuously over the years dismissed NLDC as 'heavy handed' and 'ham-handed' in its dealings with the property owners in Fort Trumbull—words that are obviously intended to prejudice the reading public against NLDC and its property acquisition actions.

"Also showing no interest in the actual process being utilized to acquire properties was The Day newspaper. *The Day* much preferred to write about 'just compensation' or 'fair market value' without any specific knowledge than to contact Dave Goebel, Jim Dunn, myself, or anyone else at or under the direction of NLDC to determine exactly how we were proceeding to acquire these properties. Again, it was much easier to refer to NLDC as 'heavy handed' or 'ham handed' rather than make an effort to provide a balanced report to its reading public. It is hard to believe that the paper continually painted a sympathetic picture of these seven property owners when they had to know they only wanted an outrageous amount of money. Also, the paper never tried to discover what process had been utilized by NLDC to determine the value of the properties, even though it subsequently turned out they were aware of it." Ariston, "A Bright Shining Lie" presented by Stephen Percy.

[33] See Chapter 114, Connecticut City and Town Development Act, *https://www.cga.ct.gov/current/pub/chap_114.htm*, and Chapter 132, Municipal Development Projects, *https://www.cga.ct.gov/current/pub/chap_132.htm#sec_8-200.*

[34] This case has generated at least two books and, recently, a movie, which portrayed Ms. Kelo as a warrior and martyr for the good of homeowners everywhere. It presents the civic leaders and players as all but engaged in a criminal conspiracy. In fact, Ms. Kelo received far more than fair compensation, had her house relocated to a nearby town, sold it, and moved to a different part of the state. See "The Little Pink House," *https://en.wikipedia.org/wiki/Little_Pink_House*; Ilya Somin, *"The story behind Kelo v. City of New London—how an obscure takings case got to the Supreme Court and shocked the nation," Washington Post,* May 29, 2015, *https://www.washingtonpost.com/news/volokh-conspiracy/wp/2015/05/29/the-story-behind-the-kelo-case-how-an-obscure-takings-case-came-to-shock-the-conscience-of-the-nation/.*

[35] See previous endnote on Connecticut City and Town Development Act.

[36] I could find none of this stated policy for its distressed cities in any of the Institute's briefings, the books written, or the erudite writings of the professor or even of his critics.

[37] *Kelo v. New London,* 268 Conn. 1, (Sup. Ct Conn.), 2004, provided the following background information:

"The record reveals the following background facts and procedural history, as aptly set forth in the trial court's comprehensive memorandum of decision. In 1978, the [NLDC] was established to assist the city in planning economic development. In January, 1998, the state bond commission authorized bonds to support planning activities in the Fort Trumbull area [of the city] and property acquisition to be undertaken by [the NLDC] in support of the project and other money toward the ultimate creation of a state park at Fort Trumbull. In February, 1998, [Pfizer, Inc. (Pfizer)] announced that it was developing a global research facility on the . . . New London Mills site which is adjacent to the Fort Trumbull area. In April, 1998, the New London city council gave initial approval to prepare a development plan for the Fort Trumbull area and the [NLDC] began holding informal neighborhood meetings regarding the [development plan] process. In May, 1998, the city council authorized [the NLDC] to proceed under chapters 130, 132 and/or 588 (l) of the [General] Statutes.

"The state bond commission approved more funds for [the NLDC] activity. In June, 1998, the city formally conveyed the New London Mills site to Pfizer. In July, 1998, a consulting team was appointed for the state Environmental Protection Act process and to prepare the [development plan]. Six alternative plans for the project area were considered as part of the required environmental impact evaluation.

"The development plan area is approximately ninety acres in size and is located on the Thames River in New London, adjacent to the proposed Fort Trumbull State Park, and the Pfizer Global Research facility, which opened in June, 2001. See Appendix to this opinion. It presently includes residential and commercial areas and is comprised of approximately 115 land parcels. The development plan area also includes the presently closed United States Naval Undersea Warfare Center, which is thirty-two acres, and also the regional water pollution control facility.

"In its preface to the development plan, the [NLDC] stated that its goals were to create a development that would complement the facility that Pfizer was planning to build, create jobs, increase tax and other revenues, encourage public access to and use of the city's waterfront, and eventually 'build momentum' for the revitalization of the rest of the city, including its downtown area." *Kelo v. New London,* 268 Conn. 1, (Sup. Ct Conn.), 2004.

[38] For a brief biography about Claire Gaudiani, see http://www.clairegaudiani.*com/AboutClaire/Pages/AboutClaire.aspx.*

[39] "Claire's vision was to improve the tax base in the City of New London, create jobs, and enhance the standard of living for all of the citizens—all through economic development with (as we all learned to say) the other side of the coin—Social Justice. The principal goal that was established very early on, was to attract a Fortune 500 company to the brown field site formerly occupied by New London Mills and the Naval Underwater Systems Center (NUWC) site at For Trumbull, now abandoned by the Navy. A total of approximately 40 waterfront acres was involved—not including Fort Trumbull itself which then Governor John Rowland said the State wanted as a State Park," Ariston, "A Bright Shining Lie" presented by Stephen Percy.

[40] "In 2000, Claire was President of both Connecticut College and of the New London Development Corporation, an organization attempting vigorously to revitalize New London's economy. The research headquarters of Pfizer Pharmaceuticals is housed in Groton, and at the time, her husband

David was the director of its research university. Over the course of several meetings, Claire encouraged George Milne Jr., a then-College trustee and the Pfizer Senior Vice President, to create a research facility across the river in New London. He agreed. The NLDC continued with their project by working to develop the surrounding area: a neighborhood of houses and a sewage facility. They did this by exercising the legal rules of eminent domain over its residents, summarily displacing them from their homes. The plot of land still remains empty. The Pfizer site has since closed." Lilah Raptopoulos, "A Partial History of Connecticut College" (2011), Self-Designed Majors Honors Papers, 3. *http://digitalcommons.conncoll.edu/selfdesignedhp/3* citing Timothy P. Carney, "Pfizer deserts its monument to corporate welfare," *Washington Examiner, November 11, 2009. http://washingtonexaminer.com/politics/pfizer-deserts-its-monument-corporate-welfare.*

[41] "Governor Dannel P. Malloy today announced an historic partnership with General Dynamics Electric Boat (ED) that will help the company grow their workforce by nearly 1,900 bringing it to more than 13,000 by 2034, allow for capital investments of greater than $800 million in the state over the next 17 years, and more than double their spending on in-state suppliers, which are located in 102 Connecticut cities and towns. Connecticut's investment will allow EB to maintain its position as the highest-quality provider of submarines to the U.S. Navy, thus capturing additional overhaul and repair work while continuing the delivery of the Virginia Class Submarines." Connecticut State Department of Economic and Community Development, "Gov. Malloy Announces Historic Long-Term Partnership with General Dynamics Electric Boat. Company to Retain and Grow Workforce to More Than 13,000 Jobs While Investing More Than $800 Million in Connecticut," State of Connecticut press release, May 1, 2018.

[42] "We—NLDC and the City of New London (although they didn't know it then and don't realize it to this day) were incredibly fortunate in having George Milne on the Board of Directors. He brought not only a global vision that rivaled and complemented Claire's, but a most business-like approach to the challenge as well as the ability to command resources far beyond the ability of NLDC to afford." Ariston, "A Bright Shining Lie" presented by Stephen Percy.

[43] "George Milne intended to place the Pfizer research facility in the city of New London; however, from the records obtained by the New London

and Hartford papers, there is no doubt that Pfizer was encouraged by Claire Gaudiani's entreaties. Also important to Pfizer were expectations of standard economic incentives, such as cost and tax breaks on the land and headquarters when built, and by anticipated state appropriations to fund the clean-up of the scrap yard, the berming of the treatment plant and the other clearance requirements so as to accommodate new offices and a nearby hotel." Ted Mann, "Bringing Pfizer to New London Came at a Heavy Cost to Taxpayers," *The Day, November 21, 2009, https://www.theday.com/article/20091121/nws12/311219912.*

[44] "Fort Trumbull neighborhood remains vacant a decade after city took land," *The Day, June 21, 2015, https://www.theday.com/local/20150619/fort-trumbull-neighborhood-remains-vacant-a-decade-after-city-took-land.*

[45] "'If Pfizer and Wyeth combine sales forces and other operations, they will have a sleeker cost structure,' said Erik Gordon, a professor at the Ross School of Business at the University of Michigan. 'Most other large companies have cut just everything they can. The only way to come up with new cuts without endangering their future is to merge in a way that creates redundancies that give the companies new job-cutting opportunities.' Two weeks ago Pfizer said it would lay off 800 researchers, and it hinted at further job cuts. Last year, it did away with more than 10,000 jobs and announced it would focus on six therapeutic areas—cancer, pain, inflammation, diabetes, Alzheimer's disease and schizophrenia." Andrew Ross Sorkin, *"Pfizer Said to be Closing in on Deal for Wyeth," The Gainesville Sun, January 24, 2009, https://www.gainesville.com/article/LK/20090124/News/604171720/GS/.*

[46] "Pfizer is wasting no time merging Wyeth into its corporate structure. The pharma giant announced its global research facility strategy on Monday, punctuated by the closing of six sites including its massive New London facility, which opened in 2001. Pfizer will end R&D operations in Princeton, NJ; Chazy, NY; Rouses Point, NY; and Plattsburgh, NY; Sanford, NC and Research Triangle Park, NC; and Gosport, England and Slough/Taplow, England. The New London staff will be transitioned to Groton, CT." George Koroneous, "Pfizer Quick on the Draw with R&D Location Plans," PharmExec.com, November 11, 2009, *http://www.pharmexec.com/pfizer-quick-draw-rd-location-plans.*

[47] Several perspectives on the New London development, the *Kelo case, and closing of the Pfizer facilities were offered in the New York Times. Editors, "A Turning Point for Eminent Domain," N.Y. Times.com, November 12, 2009, https://roomfordebate.blogs.nytimes.com/2009/11/12/a-turning-point-for-eminent-domain/.*

[48] From the standpoint of a longtime taxpayer of beach front property in the City of New London, I find it astounding that outsiders cannot appreciate the public benefits and public service that a substantial new employer brought to the area and that, but for the Institute of Justice delaying tactics, would have brought a hotel and modern office facilities in addition to the Global Headquarters as well.

[49] In this chapter, I didn't include the descriptions of the states and cases that, subsequent to the *Kelo* case, entertained or passed legislation that sought to narrow the *Berman/Kelo* Supreme Court validation of the economic development use of the eminent domain power. The exception is two cases in New York City that, in fact, broadened the use. In most states with large urban areas in distress, the changes in law that actually have passed are pyrrhic wordsmithing victories, at best.

[50] The thoughts expressed here were originally considered by me when counseling Governor Rowland in his quest to move the Patriots football team to a particular site in Hartford. To his credit, I learned that an academic professor of law has published an excellent law review about the *Kelo* case. He pointed out that the "just compensation" argument could have been made to the benefit of all the players in the Fort Trumbull matter. Clayton P. Gillette, "*Kelo* and the Local Political Process," *Hofstra Law Review* 34, no.1, Article 2.

[51] Ibid.

[52] Ibid.

[53] "The true public authority is a public corporation set up outside the regular framework of federal, state or local government, and freed from the procedures and restrictions of routine government operations, in order that it may bring the best techniques of private management to the operation of self-supporting or revenue-producing public enterprise." Jon J. Lines, Ellen L. Parker, and David C. Perry, "Building the Twentieth Century Public Works Machine: Robert Moses and the Public Authority," The Nelson A.

Rockefeller Institute of Gov't., S.U.N.Y. 22 (Fall 1986), 3 (omitting citations).

[54] "The public authority was enthusiastically adopted by many states between 1933 and 1939." Jon J. Lines, Ellen L. Parker, and David C. Perry, "Building the Twentieth Century Public Works Machine: Robert Moses and the Public Authority," The Nelson A. Rockefeller Institute of Gov't., by S.U.N.Y. 22 (Fall 1986), 5 (omitting citations).

[55] Social scientists have long abandoned the view of "project" housing in favor of mixed housing based on a formula of 80% for standard rental and 20% for rental subsidy by federal and state vouchers.

[56] The public authorities' success "was rooted in its ability to raise funds through the sale of bonds . . . this capacity to generate revenue independent of the politics of taxation allowed the public authority substantial autonomy from conventional governmental control and oversight." Jon J. Lines, Ellen L. Parker, and David C. Perry, "Building the Twentieth Century Public Works Machine: Robert Moses and the Public Authority," The Nelson A. Rockefeller Institute of Gov't., S.U.N.Y. 22 (Fall 1986), 2.

[57] More information on second injury funds is available from the Office of the Connecticut State Treasurer. See: Overview of Second Injury Fund and Frequently Asked Questions, *https://www.ott.ct.gov/secondinjury_overview.html* and *https://www.ott.ct.gov/secondinjury_faq.html.*

[58] "The spring borrowing, which grew nearly every year and helped the state make payments to school districts and local governments, is a complex transaction that essentially involved the state's lending increasing amounts to itself to pay off the previous year's loan with interest. It is perhaps the most infamous of all the measures used to achieve at least technical balance in budgets during years when the state routinely spends more money than it is taking in. The study today found that the law had been largely ineffective because it did not actually insure that the state will end any particular fiscal year without an operating deficit. Indeed, last year a gap in the budget forced the state to borrow $1 billion in a transaction that was entirely separate from the spring borrowing, and similar borrowing for about $500 million is expected this year." Sam Howe Verhovek, "Study Says 'Spring Borrowing' Ban Has Little Effect" *N.Y. Times, March 11, 1992, https://www.nytimes.com/1992/03/11/nyregion/study-says-spring-borrowing-ban-has-little-effect.html.*

[59] Hawkins prepared an informal, but detailed, memorandum that outlined the methodology to finance the state's accumulated deficits via bonds issues funded by revenues derived from the pledge of 1% of the state's sales tax.

[60] "Various issues for which Mr. Regan has been criticized [include] Mr. Regan's approval of a budget for the City of Yonkers that turned out to be unbalanced and a letter from his office endorsing investments by local governments through a broker that later became involved in a bankruptcy." Michael Oreskes, "Cuomo and Regan Split on State Fiscal Policies," *N.Y. Times, July 31, 1984.*

[61] "Edward V. Regan, a Buffalo Republican who knew little about high finance when he became the New York State comptroller but soundly managed billions in public pension funds and monitored hundreds of municipalities and state agencies for 14 years, died on Saturday in Greenwich, Conn. He went skiing in Vermont and had an aide in Albany announce his candidacy. But he despaired of fund-raising and dropped out when a seemingly formidable Mayor Edward I. Koch of New York entered the race for the Democratic nomination. Then Mario M. Cuomo beat Mr. Koch in the primary and went on to win the governorship." Robert D. McFadden, "Edward V. Regan, Longtime New York State Comptroller, Dies at 84," *N.Y. Times, October 18, 2014, https://www.nytimes.com/2014/10/19/nyregion/edward-v-regan-longtime-new-york-state-comptroller-dies-at-84-.html.*

[62] "This view of governance, which views good management and healthy profits as its epitome runs through Mr. Lhota's campaign to be mayor of New York City, and is evidenced in his background." "In the Red, Investigative Profile: Joseph Lhota, Mayoral Candidate," *https://aaaforeffort.wordpress.com/tag/twu100/.*

[63] The rating agency overlooked the basic fact that the credit card companies had "underwritten" who received their credit cards (e.g., college students) before securitization was developed to offload the risk. Meanwhile, mortgages were being "securitized" without the banks retaining any risk; they had no skin in the game.

[64] "The federal government loses money on the municipal bond tax exemption because the tax savings realized by the holders of the municipal bonds is greater than the differential between the interest yields on the tax exempt and taxable securities." Carol L. Gruendel, "The IRS's Application of Arbitrage

Provisions: Overregulation of Municipal Finance," *Fordham Urban Law* Journal 10, no. 4 (1981), fn 14 citing S. Rep. no. 552, 91st Cong., 1st Sess. 218 (1969) reprinted in 1969 U.S. Code Cong. & Ad. News 2027, 2253, available in the appendices.

[65] "Authorities are split, however, on the source of the federal tax exemption. The general view is that the tax exemption has a constitutional basis both in the reciprocal immunity doctrine and in the federal system of government under which the federal government does not interfere with the powers and affairs of local governments . . . Opponents argue . . . that the federal government does have a right to tax municipal bonds under the Sixteenth Amendment: "The Congress shall have the power to lay and collect taxes on incomes from whatever source derived. . . ." Carol L. Gruendel, "The IRS's Application of Arbitrage Provisions: Overregulation of Municipal Finance," Fordham Urban Law Journal 10, no. 4 (1981), fn 12 (internal citations omitted), available in the appendices.

[66] "The Tenth Amendment (Amendment X) to the United States Constitution, which is part of the Bill of Rights, was ratified on December 15, 1791. It expresses the principle of federalism and states' rights, which strictly supports the entire plan of the original Constitution for the United States of America, by stating that the federal government possesses only those powers delegated to it by the United States Constitution. All remaining powers are reserved for the states or the people," Wikipedia.

[67] Brief of the National Association of State Treasurers as Amicus Curiae Supporting Petitioners, at 11, *Dep't of Revenue of Ky. v. Davis,* on Writ of Certiorari to the Ct. Appeals of Ky., 2007, before the USSC.

[68] That ruling of SCOTUS also supports the state or its political subdivisions owning hotels and various other enterprises, even if managed by private entities under "so-called" qualified management contracts, which are designed as fee-based and not profit-sharing.

[69] "The multi-trillion-dollar municipal-bond market skirted a land mine Monday when the Supreme Court ruled that states could continue to give special tax breaks on the bonds that finance hospitals, roads, schools and other services." Associated Press, "Supreme Court Upholds Tax Exemptions for Municipal Bonds," *N.Y. Times, May 19, 2008, https://www.nytimes.com/2008/05/19/business/apee-bizcourt.html.*

[70] "The case centered on the practice of states granting tax exemptions to the interest on bonds issued by themselves or their subdivisions, while taxing the interest on bonds issued by others. Most states—40 of them, including Kentucky, follow this practice." John E. Petersen, columnist, "The U.S. Supreme Court expresses its fondness for muni bonds and accepts the way things are," Bond Bliss.

[71] "Kentucky's tax exemption 'favors a traditional government function.'" Associated Press, "Supreme Court Upholds Tax Exemptions for Municipal Bonds," *N.Y. Times*, May 19, 2008, *https://www.nytimes.com/2008/05/19/business/apee-bizcourt.html*

[72] For a more detailed discussion on arbitrage, see the following articles. The "ongoing debate over tax-exempt bonds usually hinges upon an unstated assumption that passes unchallenged—that a tax exemption for interest on state and local bonds is a federal subsidy to state and local governments . . . The federalism argument begins with the proposition that exemptions are not subsidies. That being so, congressional revocation of a tax exemption on interest from state and local obligations violates federalism principles to the extent it impairs a state's prerogative to borrow money—an inherent aspect of state sovereignty." Maxwell A. Miller, "The Resurgence of Federalism: The Case for Tax-Exempt Bonds, 1997," *Texas Review of Law & Politics (1997); Carol L. Gruendel, "The IRS's Application of Arbitrage Provisions: Overregulation of Municipal Finance," by Fordham Urban Law Journal 10, no. 4 (1981).*

[73] One arbitrage scheme which prompted the Treasury Department to issue the News Release . . . was described in a ruling requested by the State of Ohio. The Ohio Development Finance Commission would issue $100 million of bonds—$10 million of the bond proceeds were used for public purposes, and $90 million of the proceeds would be invested in federal securities bearing a higher interest rate than the state bonds." Carol L. Gruendel, "The IRS's Application of Arbitrage Provisions: Overregulation of Municipal Finance," *Fordham Urban Law Journal* 10, no. 4 (1981), fn 25 (internal citations omitted), available in the appendices.

[74] "A municipal sinking fund is a special fund, set apart from the other funds of an issue, which is used to retire that municipality's debt. The interest accumulated by the investment of the sinking fund is used to retire a portion of the municipality's debt. Generally, municipal obligations have serial maturities and a portion of the principal often is paid off gradually over a

long period of time through the use of a sinking fund." Carol L. Gruendel, "The IRS's Application of Arbitrage Provisions: Overregulation of Municipal Finance," *Fordham Urban Law Journal 10, no. 4 (1981), fn 52, available in the appendices.*

[75] "The Treasury Department objected to invested sinking funds because the result of this financing device was that bonds were left outstanding longer than necessary." Carol L. Gruendel, "The IRS's Application of Arbitrage Provisions: Overregulation of Municipal Finance," *Fordham Urban Law Journal 10, no. 4 (1981), fn 52, available in the appendices.*

[76] "Since the introduction of the first arbitrage restrictions in the Tax Reform Act of 1969, the Internal Revenue Service (IRS) has established a series of regulations governing municipal arbitrage. Although the IRS has sought to prevent what it considers to be arbitrage abuses, municipal issuers have successfully adapted their financing techniques to conform to the periodic changes in the regulations." Carol L. Gruendel, "The IRS's Application of Arbitrage Provisions: Overregulation of Municipal Finance," *Fordham Urban Law Journal 10, no. 4 (1981), at 662, available in the appendices.*

[77] Infrastructure projects supply jobs for the community they are located in, both during construction and operation. See Joseph Kane, "Recognizing Infrastructure's Role as a Local Economic Anchor," Brookings Institute (August 10, 2018), *https://www.brookings.edu/blog/the-avenue/2018/08/10/recognizing-infrastructures-role-as-a-local-economic-anchor.*

[78] Governor Rockefeller recognized that preservation of employment in the New York cities was vital to the economy and established similar state offices in Binghamton, Rochester, and Buffalo. "The State's Infrastructure is the cornerstone of New York's economy." Jon J. Lines, Ellen L. Parker, and David C. Perry, "Building the Twentieth Century Public Works Machine: Robert Moses and the Public Authority," The Nelson A. Rockefeller Institute of Gov't., S.U.N.Y. 22 (Fall 1986), citing Gov. Mario Cuomo Annual Budget Message 1984.

[79] *CVS Schuyler v. South Mall Constructors*, 32 A.D.2d 454 (3d Dept. 1969). See also William J. Quirk, "Albany South Mall Contractors Relief Act an Unconstitutional Infringement Upon Court of Claims Jurisdiction," *Cornell Law Review* 57, no. 1, Art 2 (Nov. 1971).

[80] Details of the first and second example are found in later chapters.

[81] Wikipedia, "Stanley S. Surrey," *https://en.wikipedia.org/wiki/Stanley_S._Surrey*

[82] "Tax subsidies constitute a form of government spending." Stanley S. Surrey and Paul R. McDaniel, "The Tax Expenditure Concept and the Budget Reform Act of 1974," *B.C. Indus. and Commer. Law Review 17, no. 5 (June 1976), https://lawdigitalcommons.bc.edu/cgi/viewcontent.cgi?referer=https://www.google.com/&httpsredir=1&article=1529&context=bclr.*

[83] "As part of his push to balance the federal budget, Obama has repeatedly suggested limiting the rate at which high-income taxpayers can reduce their liability at 28 percent. If approved, the cap would essentially drive down the appeal of municipal bonds, which are often sold to wealthy investors willing to accept lower interest rates because of the exemption. The suggestion has rattled both buyers and sellers in the $3.7 trillion bond market." Lisa Lambert, "U.S. Treasury stands behind cap on municipal bond exemption," Reuters, June 25, 2013, *https://www.reuters.com/article/municipals-exemption-idUSL2N0F113M20130625.*

[84] The Tower Amendment is a 1975 amendment to the Securities and Exchange Act of 1934.

[85] The Dodd-Frank statute as interpreted by the SEC regulations without any legislative history or other justification brought the public financial advisory profession under the regulatory oversight of the SEC. Unfortunately, it limited opportunities for creative concepts being brought to state treasurers with confidence by investments bankers, because the regulation required an independent financial advisor be in the room for the discussion. Many state treasurers objected to the SEC requiring their offices to hire an independent financial advisor since they had the expertise on staff to evaluate proposals by underwriters.

[86] Mark Pazniokas, "At 100, remembering Connecticut's 'Ella,'" *The CT Mirror, May 10, 2019, https://ctmirror.org/2019/05/10/at-100-remembering-connecticuts-ella/?utm_source=Connecticut+Mirror+Mailing+List&utm_campaign=2749f92a60-DAILY_BRIEFING_AFTERNOON&utm_medium=email&utm_term=0_571d22f8e4-2749f92a60-68206373.*

[87] See earlier chapters for discussion of public purpose.

[88] "Industrial Development Bonds (IDBs) are tax-exempt securities issued up to $10 million by a government agency to provide money for the acquisition, construction, rehabilitation and equipping of manufacturing and processing facilities for private companies." Industrial Development Bond Financing, CA.gov. *http://www.ibank.ca.gov/industrial-development-bond-financing/*.

[89] The referendum requirement was thought in 1933 to be the best way of assuring support of public works, but it proved to be a major obstacle to incurring debt for projects clearly necessary. Hence, more and more debt in New York was issued by public authorities. It was subject to appropriation of state funds if needed, making the debt a "moral obligation" but not a legal obligation of the state, thereby bypassing the referendum requirement.

[90] After his public service as treasurer, Berdon was appointed to the Supreme Court and became the maverick of that Court taking on regularly and dissenting many times from a Court which was practically dominated by my first cousin David M. Borden, the nephew of a former chief judge Abe Borden. Borden as a "conservative" Democrat and Berdon as a "liberal" Republican became a classic well-balanced court with David usually carrying the majority and, therefore, his extraordinarily well-written opinions for almost thirty years of almost every important case will stand Connecticut jurisprudence well for this century.

[91] Bob Rosenberg had become a partner in 1974 and by that time we had worked well together on many matters and had cooperated in many ways, not only on substantive matters of law, but on how to develop the bond business that was beginning to expand to new areas, such as housing finance and industrial development bonds. He had been victimized in 1972 when, as a relatively new associate assigned to the Wood-Curley-Ferdon group at Hawkins, both Curley and then Ferdon had left the firm (these departures are discussed in another chapter and derived directly from President Nixon steering bond business to his former law firm). I became his mentor and confidant until his partnership and for the rest of his much-too-short life, he and I were in daily discussions regarding management of the firm and business opportunities.

[92] Interestingly, in 1966, Bob Rosenberg and I were surprised to find out when each of us were hired that there was and had been another Jewish partner, Charles Kades. We found out when a rabbi was hired, by his waspy

third wife, for the funeral at Arlington Cemetery. Mr. Kades was the aide to General MacArthur who wrote the pacifism provisions of the post-WWII Japanese Constitution. His funeral included the full Marine Corps Band, a riderless horse, and a caisson. As we walked behind this formal procession, the Jewish funeral music "Hava Nagila" was played. Bob and I smiled at each other and realized Chuck was "coming out of the closet."

[93] Hawkins issued an opinion on February 17, 1977, which opined "(1) fee title to the land in the claim area will not be affected by the assertions being made by the Indians in the Courts, and (2) although the matter is not entirely free from doubt, a court of final jurisdiction will not grant to the Indians a right of possession and occupancy to land in the claim area."

[94] "Mr. Weicker, an outspoken opponent of casino gambling, recognized the Mohegan Tribe in eastern Connecticut as a sovereign nation and settled its land claims, and in exchange for at least $80 million a year in payments to the state, also put it in the casino business." George Judson, "Weicker Signs Agreement With 2 Tribes on Casino Gambling," *N.Y. Times, April 26, 2004, https://www.nytimes.com/1994/04/26/nyregion/weicker-signs-agreement-with-2-tribes-on-casino-gambling.html.*

[95] "Gov. Lowell P. Weicker Jr. signed agreements with two Indian tribes today that could raise the ante too high for anyone other than Indians to ever operate casinos in Connecticut." George Judson, "Weicker Signs Agreement With 2 Tribes on Casino Gambling," *N.Y. Times, April 26, 2004, https://www.nytimes.com/1994/04/26/nyregion/weicker-signs-agreement-with-2-tribes-on-casino-gambling.html.*

[96] For a more detailed overview of the status of gambling prior to Governor Schwarzenegger's election, see Aaron Peardon, "Jackpot! A legal history of Indian gaming in California," UNLV Theses, Dissertations, Professional Papers, and Capstones, 2011, *https://digitalscholarship.unlv.edu/cgi/viewcontent.cgi?article=1906&context=thesesdissertations.*

[97] By paying off all of Romania's debt, the country had no banks and creditors who therefore could decide without concern whether to lend the country any money. Ceauşescu was a known "bad guy," and his country at the time was not creditworthy because of this rule. Wikipedia, "History of Romania," Exhibit Y: "Ceausescu eventually initiated a project of total reimbursement of the foreign debt (completed in 1989, shortly before his

overthrow)," *https://en.wikipedia.org/wiki/History_of_Romania#Communist_period_(1947%E2%80%931989).*

[98] We had reason to believe his contracts were solid in that, in Bucharest, he took us to the temple where he was bar mitzvah'd, and we met his rabbi. We were told how Dr. Cohen had been instrumental in paving the way for Jewish refugees leaving Russia through Romania on their way to Israel. It was not surprising in my mind that the dictator, known for brutality to his own citizens, was willing, for a price, to allow Romania to be a way station for so many Jews in their critical passage out of Russia to Israel. As this chapter describes, Hawkins still did not get any bond business because we were not willing to pay the price (the bribe).

[99] For a case study of Robert Moses and the TBA, see Jon J. Lines, Ellen L. Parker, and David C. Perry, "Building the Twentieth Century Public Works Machine: Robert Moses and the Public Authority," The Nelson A. Rockefeller Institute of Gov't., S.U.N.Y. 22 (Fall 1986).

[100] "A so-called 'moral obligation' bond is a revenue bond which is said to be secured by a statutory 'makeup' provision which supposedly furnishes a second tier of security to the investor." Janice C. Griffith, "'Moral Obligation' Bonds: Illusion or Security?" JSTOR, *The Urban Lawyer* 8, no. 1 (1976), 58. www.jstor.org/stable/27890676.

[101] Moral obligation debt also was used in other states to some taxpayers' dismay. "Moral obligation bonds are merely a scheme used by politicians to avoid voter approval . . . the public should not pay for debt they have never approved . . . There is nothing moral about moral obligation bonds. They are simply a means by politicians of putting the public into debt without its consent." Steve Frias, "The Immorality of Moral Obligation Bonds: Return to First Principles," *The Cranston Herald, June 12, 2013,* http://cranstononline.*com/stories/the-immorality-of-moral-obligation-bonds,82913.*

[102] "The new Project Finance Agency is a complex and ingenious fiscal device which could prove helpful solving the U.D.C.'s long-term funding problems … Nevertheless, the salability of the new bonds, like those of U.D.C., depends on public confidence in the reliability of the state's 'moral obligation' backing." See "A Moral Obligation" *N.Y. Times, February 27, 1975, https://www.nytimes.com/1975/02/27/archives/a-moral-obligation.html.*

Made in the USA
Monee, IL
04 November 2026

67377559R00095